Playing with Poems

Don't worry about the wind.
Lift the window, let it in.
Fall asleep and listen hard:
the wind will tell you
where it's been!

Playing with Poems

Word Study Lessons for Shared Reading, K–2

* concepts about print

* rhythm and rhyme

* sight words

* spelling patterns

* new vocabulary

Zoë Ryder White

Heinemann
Portsmouth, NH

Heinemann
361 Hanover Street
Portsmouth, NH 03801–3912
www.heinemann.com

Offices and agents throughout the world

Library of Congress Cataloging-in-Publication Data
White, Zoë.
    Playing with poems : word study lessons for shared reading, K–2 / Zoë Ryder White.
        p. cm.
    ISBN-13: 978-0-325-01735-8
    ISBN-10: 0-325-01735-2
    1. Vocabulary—Study and teaching (Primary). 2. English language—Phonetics—Study and teaching (Primary). 3. English language—Composition and exercises—Study and teaching (Elementary). 4. Poetry—Juvenile literature. I. Title.

PE1449.W434 2008
372.46'2—dc22   2008020462

Editor: Kate Montgomery
Production: Lynne Costa
Cover design: Night & Day Design
Typesetter: Drawing Board Studios / Valerie Levy
Manufacturing: Steve Bernier

Printed in the United States of America on acid-free paper
12 11 10 09 08   VP   1 2 3 4 5

For my family: all of its many branches.

Contents

Introduction

This section describes the process through which this book came to be written and how it might be used most effectively. This book was designed for the specific purpose of presenting poems and lessons that highlight aspects of word work typically presented in early-elementary classrooms. The value of reading and discussing all types of poems with children, often, and for pure pleasure, is enormous; *Playing with Poems* is not meant to provide an exhaustive resource of poems or a yearlong poetry curriculum.

Teaching Methods

This section provides a quick overview of typical teaching methods used when interacting with shared reading poems.

Chapter 1: In the Beginning

The poems in this chapter are designed to provide opportunities for noticing and generating rhymes, practicing directionality and other early concepts of print, and understanding that a printed word holds meaning. As the chapter progresses, focus shifts to include opportunities first for simple letter recognition within a word and then for recognition of beginning and ending letter sounds. Short vowels are introduced at the end of this chapter as part of simple CVC (consonant-vowel-consonant) words. Many of the sight words that are generally taught within this time frame will be found in the poems as well, to be highlighted as teachers see fit.

Chapter 2: Moving Forward

In addition to continuing work with early concepts of print, the poems in this chapter provide opportunities for children to practice long vowels created by adding silent *e*, two-letter consonant blends, and the simple word endings *s* and *ing*. The poems also introduce the spelling patterns *all*, *ell*, *ill*; *ang*, *ing*, *ong*, *ung*; *ank*, *ink*, *onk*, and *unk*, and two-letter consonant blends *sk*, *sm*, *sp*, *st*; *fl*, *pl*, *sl*, *vl*; *dr*, *fr*, *pr*, and *tr*.

Chapter 3: Deeper In

The poems in this chapter highlight more sophisticated word patterns, such as the vowel digraphs *ai*, *ea*, *ee*, *oa*, and *oo*; the silent beginning consonants *kn* and *wr*; and the triple-letter blends *scr*, *spr*, and *str*. Children will also be able to investigate hard and soft *c* and *g*. The poems also feature examples of simple homophones and contractions as well as an introduction to compound words.

Chapter 4: Writing and Collecting Poems for Your Class

Writing poems specific to the work being done with one's own students in one's own classroom is extraordinarily fun and satisfying, and also a great way to engage students in shared reading work. This chapter describes how teachers might try writing their own poems and also encourages teachers to be perpetually on the lookout for poems that will support and engage their students.

Acknowledgments

Thank you to my students, past and present, who teach and delight me daily.

Thank you to my extraordinary colleagues at PS 321 in Park Slope, Brooklyn. Your creativity, flexibility, thoughtfulness, dedication, and integrity are a perpetual inspiration. Thank you to Principal Liz Phillips for creating such a vibrant, collegial, creative, and rigorous learning environment for all of us!

Thank you to the poets, teachers, and students who contributed poems and ideas to this book—John Allgood, Jacob Bortner-Hart, Nicole Callihan, Beth Handman, Melissa Hart, Elizabeth Heisner, Amy Ludwig VanDerwater, and Judy Katz—I am so grateful to have your voices in these pages. Thanks especially to Elizabeth for the many conversations, for lending me a wonderful batch of second graders, and for providing always honest and specific feedback. Thanks also to Amy for being my poetry pen pal, and for the immediate interest and lively participation in this project. And thank you to fabulous first-grade teacher Tom Lee for sharing his ideas about compound words.

Thank you to my wonderful teaching partner for the 2007–8 school year, Andrea Rousso, whose contributions to this book and to my teaching life are too many to name. Andrea's insight and wisdom have been a source of inspiration daily in our classroom and have caused me to rediscover and renew a commitment to making each classroom a place where every single child feels successful, stimulated, and supported. Andrea's voice and ideas are represented throughout *Playing with Poems*, and it is important that her contributions are recognized. A specific thank-you to Andrea for ideas about refocusing an unruly class, the visual reminder to help a child "keep the noises inside her head" during a lesson, the visual reminder to help a child remember how to sit calmly on the rug during a lesson, the hand signal encouraging all children to read along with the poem, the mystery sight word bag idea, the individual line-sorting activity, ideas for how to help a child recognize that his turn is over, and countless other suggestions that have helped clarify my own teaching during our year together. The year spent working with Andrea is a gift that I will treasure always.

Thank you to the classroom teachers and teaching artists who were kind enough to try out some of these poems and lessons with your students. Dana Dillon, Emily Noelle Lambert, and Susan Kellner, thank you for spending time playing with poems with your students, and thank you for your thorough feedback and great ideas!

Thank you to all of the talented people at Heinemann—to Jillan Scahill, Stephanie Turner, and Lynne Costa for answering so clearly and quickly and thoroughly my plentiful questions, to Smokey Daniels for being an always encouraging voice, and especially to Kate Montgomery for your perpetual optimism, for believing that I had a book in me more thoroughly than I did, and for sticking by me and encouraging me for years as I tried to figure out where (and what!) it was. This book would most assuredly not be here if not for you.

And of course, thank you to my wonderful husband, Paul, for all that you are. Lucky, lucky me!

Lessons at a Glance Chart

CHAPTER 1	TITLE	CONTAINS	SIGHT WORDS	LESSON	METHOD	FROM THE CLASSROOM
p. 9	Day and Night	Simple rhyme, letters *d, s, t, w*	*all, over, the, up, went, when*	Directionality	Reading together	Tips for supporting English language learners
p. 13	First Day	Simple rhyme, beginning letter sounds: *b, c, d, f, k, l, p, s, t, w*	*and, are, but, I, got, had, here, if, my, over, the, to, what, when*	Noticing rhyme	Predicting and filling in rhyming words (cloze procedure)	Predictable problems— some children are not recognizing rhyme
p. 17	Growing	Opportunities for recognizing beginning letter sounds: *b, f, m, t*	*are, for, my, or, too*	Beginning consonant letter identification	Finding the letter *b* and marking it (e.g., with colored tape)	Predictable problems— confusion between *b* and *d*
p. 22	Fox and Froggy	Opportunities for recognizing beginning letter sounds: *d, f, p, s, w*	*and, for, from, the*	We read together	Choral reading	
p. 24	Sun and Moon	Opportunities for recognizing beginning letter sounds: *b, c, d, l, m, n, p, s, t*	*and, it, of, out, the, too*	Words are discrete collections of letters	Pointing below the words	Management tips— when anxiety is keeping students from focusing
p. 28	No Nap for Me	Work with beginning and ending letter sounds, *m and n* (also *b, g, h, l, s, t, y*)	*got, how, in, me, my, no, not, of, too, I, am*	Letter identification: *m* versus *n*	Identifying and filling in the missing letter (letters covered with sticky notes)	Tips for using the missing letter method
p. 31	Feeding the Birds	Work with beginning and ending letter sounds, featuring *b* versus *d*	*an, from, in, love, my, of, our, said, the, they, to*	Letter identification: *b* versus *d*	Raising a different hand for each letter	Tips for supporting English language learners

Introduction

In 2007, I was teaching first grade. I had planned to teach the spelling patterns *ink, ank, onk,* and *unk* in word study one week, and I had been searching everywhere for a poem I might use during shared reading to highlight those sounds. I found, of course, dozens of wonderful children's poems out there in the world. But because I couldn't find a poem I liked that contained examples of the exact spelling patterns I intended to teach, I found myself walking to school creating a mental list of *ink, ank, onk,* and *unk* words. *Pink, think, wink, blink,* I thought as I walked past the twenty-four-hour laundry center and stepped over a pile of blue-wrapped *New York Times* waiting near apartment doorsteps. *Thank, blank, bank,* I thought as I waited for the light to change with a string of excited dogs attached to the hand of a sleepy early-morning dog walker. *Bonk. Bunk. Kerplunk.* On down Seventh Avenue toward PS 321, the public elementary school in Park Slope, Brooklyn, where I currently teach kindergarten. When I made my way up to my classroom, the poem "Poor Frog" was starting to take shape in my head. Certainly not a masterpiece, I thought, but adequate for my purposes! I wrote it up on chart paper and tried it out that very day on my first graders.

> **Poor Frog**
> The frog stares.
> His face is blank.
> But wait!
> I think
> I saw him blink!
> Kerplunk!
> I heard him jump!
> Bonk!
> He bumped his head
> on the log
> that is his bed.
> Poor frog!

As the weeks went on, I wrote a few more poems for my students. I started wishing that I had a sequence of poems ready to use for shared reading so that I might consistently support my word study curriculum with appropriate examples of spelling patterns and sight words. A colleague tried out some of the poems in her class and agreed that it would be great to have a collection of poems in sequence. Hence, here is *Playing with Poems: Word Study Lessons for Shared Reading.* The book was designed with working teachers (myself included!) in mind. It is meant to be a practical collection of poems to use for shared reading lessons from the very beginnings of shared reading work in kindergarten, when children are beginning to revel in wordplay, rhyme, and the joy of reading together, all the way through the more sophisticated word work of second grade. As I wrote, I realized that I wanted the sequence of poems to reflect a rich variety of voices, and I started collecting poems from teacher friends, poet friends, and older students as well.

As I wrote, I also thought more and more about the importance of poems, rhymes, and songs in my own life as a little girl. I'd bounce around the house repeating favorite A. A. Milne and Lewis Carroll poems. I'd wait for the bus at the end of our long gravel driveway on gusty spring Minnesota mornings saying nursery rhymes and singing to myself. I loved to read, reread, and memorize poems to keep in my head for lonely moments. I loved the joyful rhythm of playground clapping games and jump-rope songs, how the resonance of our little-girl voices made us somehow larger than life. I loved studying the words to "We Shall Overcome" as my first-grade class sang together with my beloved teacher, Ms. Flom. Poems have been companions and comfort for as long as I can remember—and indeed humans have been saying words together from the beginning of time in the form of chants, songs, and public recitations of all sorts. We say words together during times of both celebration and mourning. When many humans speak together the same words as one voice, a strong and joyful community is created.

It has been one of the great pleasures of my teaching life to create such community with children, through both singing together and saying poems together during shared reading. I have learned about shared reading gradually, both from my colleagues and mentors and from the field's great luminaries. Don Holdaway of course paved the way by encouraging us to cuddle our whole class up on our laps (figuratively speaking, of course!) as we read stories together. This work stands firmly on his shoulders and on the shoulders of Brenda Parkes and countless others.

Besides the clear community-building benefits of reading together, shared reading is a powerful component of any literacy program for several reasons. Each child in a classroom can enter into the shared reading process from his own level, without being called out individually. From within the safety of the great combined voice of the group, children who might be tentative about taking risks are supported in doing just that. Children who are reading more fluently not only are able to practice new word work as it is introduced but are also provided with multiple opportunities to read with expression and to discuss the ideas presented by each text. Everyone participates, and everyone succeeds. Shared reading provides multiple opportunities for teachers to model particular skill-based and comprehension-based reading strategies for children, as well as modeling reading with fluency and expression, as well as modeling the curiosity and pleasure stimulated by reading poems. Because one can present children with texts that may be well above their own independent reading levels, children have the opportunity to not only practice new reading skills but also participate in more sophisticated conversation about content and structure than might happen if discussion were limited to those texts children could read on their own. Shared reading provides many opportunities for children to notice and practice the new spelling patterns and sight words that are, of course, the organizing principle of this book. A nice byproduct of the shared reading process is that children often memorize the poems the class is studying; not only are they able to carry poems around in their heads wherever they go, but memorization is a wonderful way for students to internalize language deeply. For example, one day I heard my students Miles and Sylvie reciting a poem we'd studied together, "Backyard Digging," as they dug deep into the block box for a particular shiny plastic block. I think that the nursery rhymes and poems I memorized as a child have done as much to support the rhythm and wordplay of the poems I write now (both for adults and for children) as has the studying I have done since!

Playing with Poems is organized into four chapters, preceded by a brief description of teaching methods used within the lessons. Chapter 1, "In the Beginning," contains poems and lessons aimed toward the newest of shared reading participants. Early lessons are focused on choral reading, the wordplay of rhyme and rhythm, directionality, and letter recognition. As the chapter progresses, lessons begin to focus on letter-sound relationships and simple sight word recognition. Finally, short vowels are introduced in the form of simple CVC (consonant-vowel-consonant) words. Chapter 2, "Moving Forward," is aimed toward children who are beginning to read independently. Poems and lessons focus on the introduction of sight words, simple spelling patterns, consonant digraphs, two-letter consonant blends, the word endings s and *ed*, and, at the end of the chapter, long vowel–silent *e* words. Chapter 3, "Deeper In," presents poems and lessons for children who are comfortable reading independently and ready to do more sophisticated word work. Lessons focus on the introduction of vowel digraphs in CVVC words, triple-letter consonant blends, silent beginning letters (in *kn* and *wr*), homophones, hard and soft letters *c* and *g*, simple contractions, and compound words. Each of these chapters begins with a brief description of the teaching points commonly used during each phase of shared reading work. You'll also find a printable version of each of the poems on the Heinemann website at books.heinemann.com/white.

Each of these three chapters may roughly correspond to work done in the context of kindergarten, first grade, and second grade, but I hope for teachers to be able to pick and choose poems from each section to use as appropriate to work being done in their classrooms. Some teachers may choose to work sequentially through the book, using the lesson suggestions as they go. Some teachers may prefer to simply use the poems and design lessons tailored to the needs of their specific classrooms. Some teachers may not move sequentially through the book, but dip in and out from time to time when searching for a poem to use to teach a particular concept, sight word, or spelling pattern, using the book as a resource of texts to bolster shared reading work already being done.

Finally, Chapter 4, "Writing and Collecting Poems for Your Class," describes the process of writing one's own poems to use for shared reading, along with wholehearted encouragement to teachers to try writing poems designed for their own classes! One of my favorite parts of writing this book has been collecting poems from my colleagues and friends. Some of the guest poets appearing in this book are working poets themselves, and many are classroom teachers who took up the challenge and wrote delightful and useful shared reading poems of their own. It can be very meaningful to children to study poems that were written by important adults in their lives. Not only are these poems immediately engaging to students by sheer virtue of the fact that their teacher (or assistant principal, or brother's teacher, or music teacher, or big sister) wrote them, but bringing in poems written by familiar adults does wonders for building community within a school and providing many real-life mentors to young readers and writers.

As a poet myself, it goes without saying that I have loved creating classrooms infused with poetry that's been used for many different purposes, shared reading being an extremely important one! It is important to expose children to a wide variety of poems throughout the school year, not only in the context of shared reading but in the context of reading and writing studies of poetry, to celebrate important events in the classroom (first day of spring, rainy day), and whenever the time feels right. The poems appearing in this book were written primarily for a specific purpose—teaching sight words and spelling patterns—and will reflect that purpose. Children benefit from being exposed to a wide variety of poetry, and while I hope for the poems in this book to be engaging and interesting, and to provide solid examples of craft techniques that move beyond the sight words and spelling patterns that they include, they are not meant to provide an exhaustive representation of poetic craft, nor are they meant to be the basis for a unit of study on reading or writing poetry.

I came to classroom teaching after finishing a master of fine arts degree in poetry while working for several years through the Teachers and Writers Collaborative, a nonprofit organization in New York City that places working writers in public school classrooms to teach writing from a writer's perspective. Initially, I intended to finish my degree and teach poetry at the college level. But the years I spent in the captivating, energetic, and breathtakingly innovative classrooms of New York City happily derailed my plans. I became fascinated with the process of becoming literate—and especially fascinated with those children at the very *beginnings* of their literate lives. It has been a great joy to use poetry in my early-elementary classrooms throughout the years and to see year after year the power that reading poetry together has to not only teach and reinforce new sight words, spelling patterns, and other reading skills but also lift up and unify a classroom community. I hope that you and your students enjoy playing with poems as much as I do!

Teaching Methods

Following is a list of several ways to interact with poems during shared reading time. Some methods are best used with students at the very beginnings of shared reading work, and some are best when using the poems for more sophisticated word work. Examples of each of these methods appear in lessons or "From the Classroom" descriptions in Chapters 1–3.

Pointing Below Words: Pointing below the words helps develop children's sense of directionality, helps them learn to track print, and helps them internalize some early reading behaviors that will be of great use to them as they become readers themselves. When you read the shared reading poems to your children and with your children, it is important that you model pointing below the words. You may choose to highlight this skill by inviting individual students to come to the front of the room and take turns pointing below the words as the class reads along.

Clapping Along: Clapping along with a poem as it is read helps children internalize the poem's rhythm and helps children stay together as they read. Clapping makes a poem into a song and a dance! It involves children in the act of reading in a physical way. You can also use clapping to help children notice the syllables in words.

Circling Letters, Sight Words, or Spelling Patterns: Using markers, Wikki Stix (wax strips), or transparent colored tape to identify letters, sight words, and eventually spelling patterns in the text is a great way to reinforce concepts that you are teaching in word study and to provide opportunities for practice. Shared reading may be one of the initial areas in which you highlight letters and letter sounds with a kindergarten class. You may choose a particular beginning consonant sound yourself, say it to the class, have students guess what letter makes that sound, and then have a volunteer come to the front of the room to find that letter in the poem. You may choose to have children circle the letter using a marker, but I prefer to use wax strips that can be shaped into a circle and reused or transparent colored tape. That way you may choose to highlight a variety of letters (sight words, spelling patterns) without marking up and confusing the text. You can use this same process as children become able to identify more sophisticated letter sounds, spelling patterns, and sight words as well.

Adding in Missing Letters, Sight Words, or Spelling Patterns: Identifying a missing letter, sight word, or spelling pattern from a familiar poem can provide opportunities for children to practice hearing letter sounds and then naming and writing in the letters that are missing. It's a great way to tuck in little handwriting lessons, too. You may choose as well to use a cloze procedure and remove other words from the poem so that children must use context clues (as well as their sense of rhyme, etc.) to fill in the missing words.

Generating Words That Start with a Certain Letter: After you've asked children to identify or fill in missing letters, you may want to ask them to generate a list of words that start with that letter. This provides another opportunity for children to associate the letter and the sound it makes. It's also another collaborative effort in which children at all levels will be able to participate.

Generating Rhyming Words: You can ask the class to come up with an oral list of words that rhyme, as *listening* for rhyme always comes before noticing rhyming words visually in text. You may just spend a few moments asking your students to think of words that rhyme with a word or words in the poem. You may choose to write the list down to be built on over a period of days.

Generating Words with the Same Spelling Pattern: You can even begin this kind of list by writing just the spelling pattern on the board (or chart paper) several times over and asking children to notice what different words can be made when you add a different letter to the beginning. This will help children notice that the spelling pattern will always make the same sound, and that if they know how to read or write that spelling pattern, they can read or write many other words as well. You may want to post these kinds of lists along with the poem in your room so that children can refer back to them.

Illustrating the Poem: While illustrating a poem is not something you'll ask your students to do with each poem you study together during shared reading, it can be a nice way to assess and enhance their comprehension of the poem. Certain poems might contain imagery that lends itself well to illustrations or certain figurative language that can be understood more thoroughly through re-creating it on paper.

Reading the Poem in Parts: It can be fun (and another engaging way to read together) to divide the poem into parts and have different groups of students read different lines or stanzas. This works best with poems that contain distinct sections or voices. Reading this way can add a layer of understanding to children's reading, and it also provides opportunities for them to track the text silently while they are waiting for their turn to read—a crucial skill for young readers to develop.

Acting Out the Poem: Acting out the poem in small groups or as a whole class provides a kinetic way to bring the poem to life. Children love to act things out, and acting out the poems builds a sense of community and helps develop fluency and pacing as well.

Memorizing and Reciting the Poem: Many children will memorize the shared reading poems you study just through the repetition of reading and examining the poems together as a class. You may take this one step further and have children memorize and recite poems to the class. Recitation was once an important part of literacy education, and it can be a wonderful confidence builder as well as a way to practice fluency and expression!

Extending the Poem's Pattern: Some poems lend themselves well to being extended upon by a class. Particularly if the poem you are studying has a distinct pattern—such as the repetition of "We will go" in the poem of that title—you can ask your students to come up with additional lines that fit the pattern. Not only does this process create a sense of ownership, but children practice both reading and writing as they add new lines to the poem. Even if the teacher adds the words herself, children are generating new text that fits a pattern, and they are tracking as the teacher writes. They will also love studying the poem extension that they created themselves!

Write a Class Poem Inspired by the Shared Reading Poem: Sometimes a poem may not be built around a clear pattern of sight words, but the content may lend itself well to creating a class poem based on the same idea. You may choose to encourage your class to use the same spelling patterns or sight words highlighted in the initial poem, or you may simply give the group a line to use as a launch. For example, if you are asking the children to write a poem inspired by "Wind," you may ask them to start off each line with "Wind is like . . ." and have them fill in the blank.

Using Magnetic Letters to Make Words: This is a variation on generating lists of words using the same spelling pattern. Instead of writing words on a chart, you may want to have children come to the front of the room and make words using magnetic letters. This also works with sight words.

Word Family Sorts Based on Poem: Instead of simply having children write words using various related spelling patterns in the appropriate columns of a chart, it can be fun to have them sort prepared word cards into the appropriate columns. You can do this as a whole-class activity, and you can also create small versions of the sorting activity and ask children to work individually or in partnerships to sort the words into the appropriate columns.

Poems in the Pocket Chart: Write each line of a poem on a sentence strip and have students arrange the lines in order in a pocket chart. You can also have students do this work on their own, using printed copies of the poem that children can cut line by line and glue down in order on another sheet of paper.

Mystery Sight Word Bag: Choose several sight words from the poem you are studying and write each on an index card. Put the index cards in a bag; a brown paper lunch bag works just fine. With great excitement and ceremony, shake the bag and invite children to come up and choose (no peeking!) a word from the mystery bag. Ask the child to read the word and then match it up with the word in the poem. If the word appears multiple times, the student can move the card from place to place as he matches it up with each appearance. Then continue to ask other children to come up one by one, take another word from the mystery bag, and match it to the poem.

In the Beginning

Even children at the very beginnings of their literate lives can (and must!) delight in the wordplay provided by poems, songs, and the big books used by many teachers. Early shared reading work provides ample opportunities for oral language development through a nonthreatening, community-building reading activity. Children not only practice reading, or saying the words of the poems along with the teacher together, but also have opportunities to discuss the poem's meaning and things they notice on their own about the words or letters in the poem. Children in this phase of shared reading are developing their phonemic awareness skills—the ability to identify and isolate sounds in words. Multiple readings of a poem (along with teacher guidance) help children develop fluency, expression, and intonation. The poems in this chapter are designed to provide opportunities for noticing and generating rhymes, practicing directionality and other early concepts of print, and understanding that a printed word holds meaning. As the chapter progresses, focus shifts to include opportunities first for simple letter recognition within a word and then for recognition of beginning and ending letter sounds. Short vowels are introduced at the end of this chapter as part of simple CVC words. Many of the sight words that are generally taught within this time frame will be found in the poems as well, to be highlighted as teachers see fit.

The poems themselves appear in a sequence that might be followed poem by poem in classrooms where children are new to this work—kindergarten and early first grade—or you may decide to pick and choose which poems to incorporate when into your class' shared reading work. You'll also find a bulleted list of lesson ideas broken down in sequence for each poem, with one lesson fleshed out more fully for each poem. You may decide not to go through the entire sequence of lessons for each poem but rather to pick relevant ideas. A more complete description of each of the potential teaching points provided by these poems follows. The poems can also provide opportunities for more sophisticated word work that is not highlighted here, and they can be used as you see fit to meet the needs of your particular class.

An important point to mention about the poems used for very early shared reading work is the use of picture cues. Early readers rely heavily on picture cues. While reading together provides a great deal of support to early readers, it is important to consider adding pictures to the poems you write up on chart paper, to

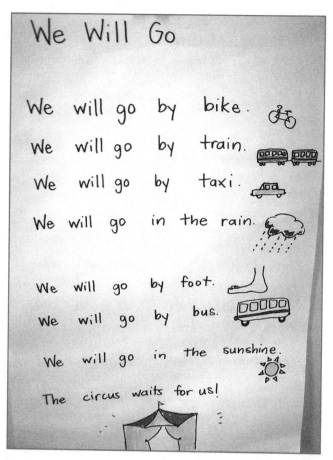

Figure 1–1 *An illustrated chart of the poem "We Will Go"*

add another level of support for your students. I often continue this practice even when children become more independent in their reading. Pictures are comforting and provide anchors in the text for young readers who may lose their place. Either drawing simple pictures yourself or using clip art to add a few simple illustrations to your shared reading poems can be invaluable to helping your children feel confident and ready to read. (See Figures 1–1 and 1–2.)

■ Sight Words Appearing in This Chapter's Poems

a, about, all, am, an, and, are, at, be, but, by, can, for, friend, from, go, got, had, has, he, her, here, his, how, I, if, in, is, it, like, love, me, much, my, no, not, of, off, on, or, our, out, over, said, so, the, they, to, too, took, up, we, went, what, when, will, with, up, you, your

■ Opportunities for Phonemic Awareness Development

letter identification
beginning and ending consonant letter-sound identification
common confusions: *b* versus *d, m* versus *n, d* versus *w*

Figure 1–2 *An illustrated chart of the poem "Pretend"*

■ Spelling Patterns Appearing in This Chapter's Poems

am, ap, at
og, op, ot
eg, en, et
ug, un, ut
ig, ip

■ Mining Poems for Teaching Points: Curricular Goals Associated with Beginning Shared Reading Work

While the curricular goals are introduced in a sequence that many teachers might choose to follow, the sequence is certainly not set in stone. You might choose to focus on sight words before focusing on spelling patterns, for example, or you might choose not to spend time on sight words at all from a particular poem. You also might focus a couple of lessons on the same curricular goal, especially if your students seem to need more time. Pick and choose what makes sense for *your* class.

Introductory Work

Poems commonly used at the beginning stages of shared reading will provide opportunities for children to hunt for letters that make certain sounds as well as some simple sight words, but those are not the things to focus on right away. Simply practicing reading together and following the teacher's pointing finger (or pencil or wand or whatever you prefer to use) is very important work for children who have not yet had much exposure to print in the context of school. Nothing is accomplished by skipping crucial steps in an attempt to hurry forward to letter recognition and sight words. Trust that along with the enjoyment children find in chorally reading the text, they are also absorbing fundamental prereading skills—directionality, the concept that letters make words, the concept that words hold meaning, and so on.

When you introduce the poems in this chapter to your students, ask them to be listeners the first time you read. At this stage, it is helpful for children to simply listen and watch as you read a new poem before they attempt to repeat the poem with you. It will not take long for children to absorb the words of the simple texts, but their understanding will be clarified if they simply take it in the first time you read it. You may want to ask them to respond to the meaning of the poem or ask them if it reminds them of anything, but keep your questions meaning based rather than print based as you introduce new poems.

After the children have listened to you read the poem once or twice through and you have discussed its meaning, invite them to join you as you read it again. Encourage them to match their voices to your voice and to your finger as it points below each word.

Focus on Comprehension

Shared reading can be used to accomplish many different teaching goals having to do with prereading and reading skills and word work. It is important to keep in mind that in addition to these sorts of goals, we also need to teach students that meaning making is the main point of reading. It is always important, whether your students are at the very beginnings of their literate lives or able to do more sophisticated word work, that the poems they read during shared reading time *mean* something. The simple poems may not have deep or sophisticated meanings, but they will all (as every text does) provide opportunities for you to monitor and enhance your students' comprehension. You may choose to simply discuss the poems and what they remind children of. You may choose to focus on images, on the sequencing of events in the poem, on unpacking the figurative language. You may choose to focus on helping your students envision the world of the poem. However you choose to approach comprehension, it's important to approach it, and to approach it early in the week so that the word work you may do later in the week is based on a foundational understanding of the poem's meaning.

Building Confidence and Community Through Choral Reading

The choral reading on which shared reading is based works toward accomplishing many curricular goals, not least among them building confidence and a sense of community. As you read and reread together, children who are both less advanced and less confident will be swept up in the rhythm and sounds of the class' voices. Reading together provides a safe forum for trying out reading skills and behaviors that children may feel timid about trying alone. Multiple opportunities to read the same poem together will allow children chances to gradually correct their reading of the poem; they will learn from hearing you read, and they will learn from the voices of their classmates. Humans have been saying words together in some form or other (chanting, singing, reading) forever, and this practice continues to be a way to align and center a group of people—as you read together, you become a clearly defined *we*, which helps develop the sense of strong community that is essential to our work as educators.

Focus on Directionality

Developing a sense of directionality is an important early shared reading goal. Through multiple opportunities to observe you pointing below words as you read the shared reading poems (left to right, top to bottom), and by having opportunities to come and point themselves as the class reads, children will begin to internalize the directionality of reading. As your students become readers themselves, you will need to highlight directionality less and less in your shared reading lessons, but it is a primary focus early on.

Focus on Words as Discrete Collections of Letters

Searching for the *repeating words* in a poem (if there are repeating words) can draw children's attention to the fact that words are discrete collections of letters that always look and sound the same—a crucial concept for children to master early on in the reading process and one that paves the way for all subsequent work. If children see what appears to be a random scramble of shapes and lines when they look at text, many of your teaching points will not hit home for them. Many children begin to internalize the way letters are organized into words without much direct teaching. Some children benefit from multiple opportunities to practice seeing words as discrete collections of letters. Using poems that contain several repeating words helps children recognize the pattern of letters in words visually—especially if the words appear next to each other or above and below each other—and connect what they see with what they hear when the poem is read. They will notice, for example, that the word *day* looks and sounds the same every time it occurs in a poem.

Focus on Developing an Ear for Rhyme

Developing the capacity to recognize and generate rhyming words will serve children well as they become readers. It paves the way for subsequent recognition and use of spelling patterns. At this early stage, the work that you do with rhyming will focus primarily on sound rather than the visual recognition of letter combinations. It is likely that more children will initially be able to *hear* rhymes that occur in the poems than will be able to see them in the text, especially if the rhyming words are not placed right next to each other. Identifying rhyming words both orally and visually is another way to help children understand that words are discrete collections of letters; it is also a precursor to identifying and learning various spelling patterns. Early on, focusing on sound will develop children's ear for rhyme and set them up for later work.

Focus on Letter Identification

When you feel that many children in your class will be able to identify some simple consonant sounds in the text of the poems you study together during shared reading, you may choose to spend some time (after reading the poem through together) asking children to come up to the chart paper and point to (or circle or put tape over) certain letters. You may ask children to find letters by name ("Hands up if you think you can find an *s* in this poem.") or by sound ("Can anyone come find a letter in this poem that makes the /s/ sound?") depending on your students' comfort level. You will want to ask children to find beginning consonant sounds first and then ending consonant sounds. Early on in the process there is no need to focus on vowel sounds, as children are not as likely to be able to hear and identify those sounds. You might also leave out letters in a poem and have individuals come up and fill them in.

Focus on Spelling Patterns

Early on in the shared reading process, children are not ready to pay attention to spelling patterns within words. Toward the end of this stage, you may start working with your students on short-vowel sounds and some simple short-vowel spelling patterns in CVC words. Some children may simply recognize that words that end the same way sound the same way; they may focus more on the rhymes they can hear. Some children will also be able to identify spelling patterns visually.

Focus on Sight Words

As you begin to study simple sight words in your classroom, shared reading can be a wonderful way to reinforce the work you have begun in word study. Encouraging children to notice and point out sight words found within shared reading poems helps children identify the new words in a meaningful context. They benefit from the teacher and peer support of shared reading as well. Even children who are not ready to identify new sight words on their own will be able to come find the words in the context of the shared reading poems.

The Poems

"Day and Night"
>   poem containing simple rhyme, letters *d, s, t, w*
>   sight words: *all, over, the, up, went, when*

"First Day"
>   poem containing simple rhyme, beginning letter sounds *b, c, d, f, k, l, p, s, t, w*
>   sight words: *and, are, but, I, got, had, here, if, my, over, the, to, what, when*

"Growing"
>   poem containing opportunities for recognizing beginning letter sounds: *b, f, m, s, t*
>   sight words: *are, for, my, or, too*

"Fox and Froggy," by John Allgood

poem containing opportunities for recognizing beginning letter sounds: *d, f, p, s, w*

sight words: *are, for, my, or, too*

"Sun and Moon"

poem containing opportunities for recognizing beginning letter sounds: *b, c, d, l, m, n, p, s, t*

sight words: and, *it, of, out, the, too*

"No Nap for Me"

poem containing work with beginning and ending letter sounds, *m* versus *n* (also *b, g, h, l, s, t, y*)

sight words: *got, how, in, me, my, no, not, of, too*

"Feeding the Birds"

poem containing work with beginning and ending letter sounds, *b* versus *d*

sight words: *an, from, in, love, my, of, our, said, the, they, to*

"Wind"

poem containing work with beginning and ending sounds, *w* versus *d*

sight words: *about, all, and, be, can, from, if, in, is, it, the, up, will, you, your*

"I Am a Ghost," by Melissa Hart

poem containing sight words: *a, am, can, I, you*

"Pretend"

poem containing work with beginning sounds: *b, f, j, l, p, q, w, y;* and ending sounds *d, f, n*

sight words: *a, am, I*

"We Will Go"

poem containing work with beginning and ending sounds: *b, f, g, n, r, s, t, w*

sight words: *by, for, go, in, the, us, we, will*

"Sam's Map"

poem containing short-vowel spelling patterns: *am, ap, at*

sight words: *a, and, at, friend, he, his, my, the, with*

"Bored"

poem containing short-vowel spelling patterns: *og, op, ot*

sight words: *a, at, his, in, on, the, with*

"Wren"

poem containing short-vowel spelling patterns: *eg, en, et*

sight words: *a, and, be, can, for, get, her, in, like, me, my, off, on, said, the, took, you*

"Picnic"
poem containing short-vowel spelling patterns: *ug, un, ut*
sight words: *a, has, in, is, much, so, the, up, we*

"Backyard Digging"
poem containing short-vowel spelling patterns: *ig, ip*
sight words: *a, is, my, or*

Day and Night

Beginning consonants: *d, s, t, w*
Sight words: *all, over, the, up, went, when*

> ### Day and Night
> The sun went up,
> the sun went down.
> The children slept
> all over town.

Curricular Goals for "Day and Night"

Following is a list of possible curricular goals to be accomplished with this poem. You need not spend a lesson on each goal. Devote your lessons to meeting those curricular goals that will best serve your particular class.

- introductory work
- focus on comprehension
- building confidence and community
- focus on directionality
- focus on words as discrete collections of letters
- focus on developing an ear for rhyme
- focus on letter identification
- focus on sight words (only if you've begun this work in word study)

We Read Together: A Lesson Using "Day and Night"

Primary Curricular Goals

- building confidence and community
- focus on directionality

Setup

- Gather your students together on the rug or at your class' meeting place so that they will all be able to see the words of the poem.
- Have your pointer available!

Introduction

- Tell your students that you will be looking at a poem together. If this is an early shared reading experience, tell them that a poem is a small piece of writing that sometimes (but not always) rhymes and that can tell a little story or help people think about the world in a new way. Explain that you will read the poem first and that they will be listeners, and that they will then have a chance to say the poem with you.

- Encourage them to watch you point below each word as you read.

Interacting with the Text

- Check your students' comprehension by asking a few questions.

- Read the poem aloud yourself once more.

- Invite your students to read with you. Let them know that they need not read (or say) all of the words. There will be a variety of levels represented, especially in early readings.

- Read the poem together again, and encourage your students to say the words all together. You may also ask children to try to say a few more words the second time than they did the first time.

From the Classroom: Tips for Supporting English Language Learners

Many of the children in the following example are English language learners and need some extra support with comprehension. By nature, the choral reading involved in shared reading will support children who are just trying out and gaining confidence with English, but even if your ELLs are able to say some or most of the words of the poem, they may not fully comprehend it. Visual cues such as the little cutout sun and sleeping child this teacher uses will support them as you read together (these kinds of cues support students with language-processing issues as well!). (See Figure 1–3.)

Tim has introduced "Day and Night" to his kindergartners by reading it through twice and then asking them what is happening in the poem. While many children have a clear understanding, Tim can see that several of his English language learners are silent and looking puzzled. He decides to take out the little cutout paper sun he has made and the picture of the sleeping child. He tells the class that this time he will be using pictures to make sure that everyone can see what is happening in the poem. He reads it again, this time lifting the sun when he reads, "The sun went up," putting it on his lap when he reads, "the sun went down," and taking out the picture of the sleeping child when he reads, "The children slept / all over town."

Figure 1–3 *Asa and Jake use picture supports with "Day and Night."*

He encourages the children to read with him the next time. He asks Sharif, who has demonstrated clear comprehension already, to be the puppeteer and use the sun and sleeping child pictures as the class reads so that he can keep pointing below the words.

"OK, everyone, let's read together this time. Sharif will be showing us with the pictures what is happening in the poem as we read. Are you ready, Sharif?" Sharif beams and nods vigorously.

"The sun went up," read Tim and the class. Tim reads slowly this time and makes eye contact with Lakshmi and Julio to see that they are watching the sun go up in Sharif's hands. It is more important for them to follow the visual cues at this point than to track the words on the page.

"What happened, Lakshmi?" asks Tim in a stage whisper.

Lakshmi grins and whispers back, "Sun up!" pointing to the ceiling.

Tim nods and the class reads, "The sun went down." Sharif vigorously drops his hands so that the sun flaps against his legs. A few children giggle. Tim smiles and stage whispers, "Julio, what happened now?"

Julio says, "Sun!" and points to the carpet.

"The children slept / all over town," reads the class. Sharif drops the sun on the floor and holds up the picture of the sleeping child.

Through his questions during the lesson, and through a quick check-in just after shared reading, Tim can see that both Lakshmi and Julio understand more of the poem than they did before.

Extending Your Class' Work with "Day and Night"

■ As a comprehension exercise (and assessment opportunity), have your students draw pictures to go along with the poem. First have a conversation with them about what elements of the poem they could make into pictures; there are three clear images that kindergartners could draw, even if they are still gaining control over the pen! Some children may identify and draw a picture of the sun going up. Some may draw the sun going down. Some may draw children tucked in bed. Some may choose to combine some variation of these images. Any of these is a fine way to illustrate the poem and a nice way to check that your kids understand it. You can hang the poem on chart paper in your room or on a bulletin board and surround it with the children's illustrations. (See Figure 1–4.)

■ Divide your class in thirds on the rug. Have the first third say the first line, "The sun went up." You may ask them to do a simple arm motion to show the sun rising. Have the second third say the second line, "the sun went down," with appropriate arm motion. The last group of children can say the last two lines, "The children slept / all over town."

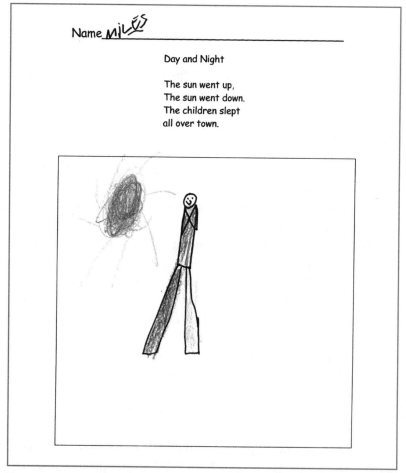

Figure 1–4 *Miles' illustration of "Day and Night"*

First Day

Beginning consonants: *b, c, d, f, k, l, p, s, t, w*
Sight words: *and, are, but, got, had, here, I, if, my, over, the, to, what, when*

> **First Day**
> I didn't want to come today.
> I hid under my bed.
> What if I cry? What if I fall?
> What if I bump my head?
> What if the kids are mean to me?
> What if no one smiles?
> What if the lunchroom ladies
> have teeth like crocodiles?
> When I walked to school, I pulled my hood
> way down over my eyes.
> But when I got here and met my friends,
> I had fun! Surprise!

Curricular Goals for "First Day"

Following is a list of possible curricular goals to be accomplished with this poem. You need not spend a lesson on each goal. Devote your lessons to meeting those curricular goals that will best serve your particular class.

- introductory work
- focus on comprehension
- building confidence and community
- focus on directionality
- focus on developing an ear for rhyme
- focus on letter identification
- focus on sight words (only if you've begun this work in word study)

Listening for and Predicting Rhyme: A Lesson Using "First Day"

Primary Curricular Goals

- focus on words as discrete collections of letters
- focus on developing an ear for rhyme

Previously Covered

- introductory work
- focus on comprehension
- building confidence and community
- focus on directionality

Setup

- Gather your students together on the rug or at your class meeting place so that they will all be able to see the words of the poem.
- Have your pointer available!

Introduction

- Tell your students that you will be continuing your work with the poem "First Day." (In previous lessons, you will have focused your teaching on comprehension and directionality as well as providing multiple opportunities for children to read the poem aloud with you.)

- Tell your students that after you read the poem aloud for them, you will be asking them to read along with you, but that they will be asked just to predict and fill in the missing rhyme. Then you'll read the poem a second time together, and the children will be asked to try to say all of the words along with you.

Interacting with the Text

- Read the poem through once on your own, asking children to follow your pointer with their eyes as they listen.
- Read the poem through again, this time pausing before each rhyming word and asking your students to say that word out loud:

  Teacher: "What if I bump my . . ."
  Students: "Head!"

- Tell your students that the next time they read with you, they will be invited to say *all* of the words along with you, and that they can use the rhyming words they know so well to help them stay together.

From the Classroom: Predictable Problems— Some Children Are Not Recognizing Rhymes

Some children, especially those whose lives have been infused with literacy-based experiences, come quite naturally to recognizing, hearing, predicting, and even generating rhyme. Some children need more direct support. In the following classroom example, Elena notices, as she predicted from informal assessments of her students, that a group of them are not supplying the missing rhyme with the rest of the class. Whether this is an issue of comprehension, attention, or unfamiliarity with rhyme, Elena cannot tell at this point. She decides to proceed under the assumption that the children could use more practice and support with rhyme, and instead of moving quickly into a read-through of the poem during which she asks the children to say all of the words along with her, she decides to provide them with more explicit rhyming support.

Elena has read the poem once through and has invited her students to supply the missing rhymes in the second read-through of the poem. Noticing that a substantial group of children has remained silent, Elena decides to take a little detour in her lesson.

"Before we go on and read all of the words of 'First Day' together, let's stop and pay attention to the rhyming words we're thinking about here. I'm going to say some pairs of words. Just listen really carefully as I say them. When you hear me say a pair of words that rhyme (or sound the same), put two thumbs up. When you hear me say a pair of words that don't rhyme (or don't sound the same), put two thumbs down. Listen carefully! The first pair of words is *bed* and *ball*. *Bed* and *ball*. Thumbs up if you think they rhyme; thumbs down if you think they don't."

Elena notices a few children looking closely around them and then deciding which way to point their thumbs—this is fine! Peer support is one of the great benefits of shared reading. When all of the thumbs are pointing down, Elena congratulates her class and moves on to the next pair.

"Let's try another. Listen carefully! *Bed* and *head*. *Bed* and *head*. Thumbs up if they sound the same; thumbs down if they don't."

The same children look around before putting up their thumbs. Once again, Elena congratulates the class. She goes through a few more pairs of words, focusing only on words that rhyme with *bed* so that the kids who need support get focused practice with one particular sound. She notices that these children are using their peers less and less as they practice. When they go back to reading the poem through together again, she keeps an eye on the children who remained silent the first time through and is happy to see that more of them are able to join in.

Extending Your Class' Work with "First Day"

■ If your students seem to be catching on quickly to the concept of rhyming words, you may ask them to generate a list of words that sound like any or all of the rhyming words in the poem. It makes sense to start with the simpler sounds first: *head* and *bed*. You may write the words up in front of them if you feel that this will be meaningful to them, or you may choose to just keep a record for yourself for assessment purposes.

■ Ask your students to draw about their own experience of the first day of school. You may provide a paper divided in half with "Before the first day" on one side and "After the first day" on the other. Ask your students to draw how their feelings have changed. Mention, of course, that some children's feelings may not have changed if they were not nervous about coming to school!

Growing

Beginning consonants: *b, f, m, t*
Sight words: *are, for, my, or, too*

> **Growing**
> My feet are too big
> for my old blue boots.
> Or are my old blue boots
> too small?

Curricular Goals for "Growing"

Following is a list of possible curricular goals to be accomplished with this poem. You need not spend a lesson on each goal. Devote your lessons to meeting those curricular goals that will best serve your particular class.

- introductory work
- focus on comprehension
- building confidence and community
- focus on directionality
- focus on letter identification
- focus on sight words (only if you've begun this work in word study)

Beginning Consonant Sounds: A Lesson on Finding b in "Growing"

Primary Curricular Goal

- focus on letter identification

Previously Covered

- introductory work
- focus on comprehension
- building confidence and community
- focus on directionality

Setup

■ Gather your students together on the rug or at your class meeting place so that they will all be able to see the words of the poem.

■ Have your pointer available as well as your choice of materials for the children to use when marking the letter *b* in the text (transparent colored tape, wax strips, or marker).

Introduction

■ Tell your students that because they have gotten to know the poem "Growing" so well by now, today you will be searching for just one letter: the letter that makes the /b/ sound.

■ Tell them that first they will listen to you read, paying attention to words that start with the /b/ sound. Remind them not to say the name of the letter out loud, just to think it, because you want everyone to have a chance to think about it at her own speed.

Interacting with the Text

■ Ask your students to listen as you read and to follow along with their eyes as you point. Ask them to pay special attention to words that start with the /b/ sound.

■ Ask your students to turn and whisper in their neighbor's ear what letter they think makes the /b/ sound.

■ Ask a student to share his guess about what letter makes that sound.

■ Invite your students to read with you, paying attention to the words with the letter *b*.

■ Ask for volunteers to come up to the poem and mark one *b* in the poem (using marker, wax strips, or transparent tape—your choice). Two or three volunteers should be sufficient.

■ You may choose to read the poem through once more together, exaggerating the /b/ sound as you read for those children who need more support.

From the Classroom: Predictable Problems— Confusion between b and d

It would be a great surprise if many children did not confuse lowercase *b* and *d*—it just goes with the territory as children begin to learn and internalize the lowercase letters. Confusion about *b* and *d* can continue well into first grade. It is quite common, when individuals come up to search for the *b*, for them to point to a *d* instead. Because this poem contains both, it provides an opportunity for children to practice noticing the difference! In the following example, Sylvan is unsure about which is *b* and which is *d* when he comes up to mark the letter. Instead of merely correcting him, I decide to use the opportunity he has provided to support the whole class.

Sylvan beams as he approaches the board to find the letter *b*. He studies the text and points enthusiastically toward the *d* in the word *old*. I ask him to take a look at the lowercase *b* in our alphabet chart to see if the bump in the word he has chosen is pointing the same way as the lowercase *b* next to the picture of a ball. He studies the chart, looks back at the letter he's pointing to, and changes his aim to point at the *b* in *blue*. I hand him a wax strip and he circles the *b*. I thank him and tell him he may go back to his rug spot.

When he sits back down, I say to the class as I point to the letter he circled, "Sylvan found the letter *b* in the word *b-b-blue* [it is nice to exaggerate the sounds you are focusing on to help children hear them and make a visual connection simultaneously], but he also reminded me of something else important this poem can help us with. Lowercase *b* and lowercase *d* look so much alike, it can be hard to figure out which is which—right, Sylvan?" The boy smiles and nods. "At first Sylvan was pointing to a *d*, but then he checked to see if the bump was on the same side as the *b* on our alphabet chart, and he figured out that he was pointing at a *d* instead. So he looked and found a *b* over here, in the word *blue*. Good work, Sylvan."

I decide to give the kids a little extra practice with lowercase *b*; throwing in a quick, impromptu handwriting lesson never hurts.

"Let's practice something before I ask for another volunteer to come up to the poem. I'm going to draw two handwriting lines below the poem, here, and I want to show you the difference between *b* and *d*."

I model each and ask the children to watch. After I model each letter, I invite the children to write the letters in the air with me for practice. Because children at this stage are just learning to distinguish left from right, I always couple those terms with a landmark in the room to help them internalize the concept.

"Remember, when we make lowercase *b*, like in the word *blue*, we make the bump on the right side of the line—the side that's closest to the classroom door. In a *d* the bump is on the left side, closest to the windows."

When I ask the next two volunteers to come up, I notice that they refer to the ABC chart as Sylvan did and are able to successfully locate and circle the *b*'s.

Extending Your Class' Work with "Growing"

■ You may ask children to think of words that start with the same sound as the letter you've focused your shared reading work on. For example, if you've asked children to identify the letter in the poem that makes the /b/ sound and several individuals have come up and circled a *b*, you may then

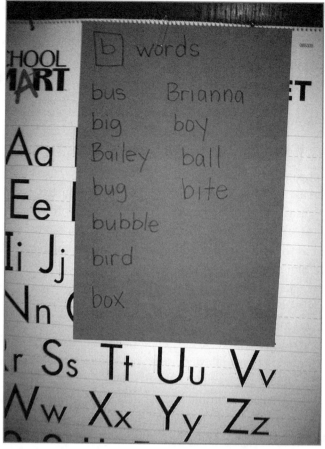

Figure 1–5 *A list of b words generated by class K-136*

ask them to think of other words that start with that letter. You do not, early in the year, need to write them down in front of the kids. You may want to keep your own record for assessment purposes. If you do choose to write a list of words in front of the kids, you may want to draw their attention to the way the *b* is formed and tuck in a bit more prehandwriting language. (See Figure 1–5.)

■ Have your students draw a picture of a favorite item of clothing that they have grown out of. (See Figure 1–6.)

Name OLIⱯVIA

Growing

My feet are too big
for my old blue boots.
Or are my old blue boots
too small?

Figure 1–6 *Olivia drew her favorite too-small sparkly
sneakers with the cool black soles.*

Fox and Froggy

Beginning consonants: *d, f, p, s, w*
Sight words: *and, for, from, the*

> ### *Fox and Froggy*
> Fee Fi Fo Fum
> Froggy plays the fiddle
> Fox frolics for fun.
> Fast water, freezing water
> Flows downstream—
> Fox and Froggy
> Flee from the scene.
> —*John Allgood*

Curricular Goals for "Fox and Froggy"

Following is a list of possible curricular goals to be accomplished with this poem. You need not spend a lesson on each goal. Devote your lessons to meeting those curricular goals that will best serve your particular class.

- introductory work
- focus on comprehension
- building confidence and community
- focus on directionality
- focus on words as discrete collections of letters
- focus on developing an ear for rhyme
- focus on letter identification
- focus on sight words (only if you've begun this work in word study)

We Read Together: A Lesson Using "Fox and Froggy"

Primary Curricular Goals

- building confidence and community
- focus on directionality
- focus on words as discrete collections of letters

Previously Covered

- introductory work
- focus on comprehension

Setup

- Gather your students together on the rug or at your class meeting place so that they will all be able to see the words of the poem.
- Have your pointer available!

Introduction

- Tell your students that you will be reading the poem through once first, and they will have two jobs as you read. One job will be to listen to the words of the poem, and the other job will be to follow along with their eyes as you point. After they listen to you read, you'll all read together, and everyone will work on saying the same words at the same time.

Interacting with the Text

- Read the poem once through, pointing below the words. Check periodically to see that each child is watching with her eyes. Remind them as necessary.

- Invite your students to read with you, asking them to try to say the words of the poem at the same time, so that their reading sounds like one big voice.

- Read through the poem together, stopping as need be to remind children to say the poem's words at the same time. You may want to exaggerate the poem's rhythm with your own voice and to point dramatically with your pointer.

- Read the poem through a second time with the same goal in mind.

Sun and Moon

Beginning consonants: *b, c, d, l, m, n, p, s, t*
Sight words: *and, it, of, out, the, too*

> ### Sun and Moon
> The sun
> the sun
> the sun
> the sun:
> it brings day
> to everyone.
>
> The moon
> the moon
> the moon
> the moon:
> small light
> of the night,
> please come
> out soon.

Curricular Goals for "Sun and Moon"

Following is a list of possible curricular goals to be accomplished with this poem. You need not spend a lesson on each goal. Devote your lessons to meeting those curricular goals that will best serve your particular class.

- introductory work
- focus on comprehension
- building confidence and community
- focus on directionality
- focus on words as discrete collections of letters

- focus on developing an ear for rhyme
- focus on letter identification
- focus on sight words (only if you've begun this work in word study)

Pointing Below the Words: A Lesson Using "Sun and Moon"

Primary Curricular Goals

- focus on directionality
- focus on words as discrete collections of letters

Previously Covered

- introductory work
- focus on comprehension
- building confidence and community

Setup

- Gather your students together on the rug or at your class meeting place so that they will all be able to see the words of the poem.
- Have your pointer available!

Introduction

- Tell your students that because they know the poem "Sun and Moon" so well now, after they practice reading the poem with you once, some of them will have a chance to come up and practice "being the teacher" and pointing below the words of the poem as the class reads along.

Interacting with the Text

- Read the poem once through, pointing below the words. Ask your students to follow along with their eyes as you read.

- Read the poem again, pointing below the words. Ask your students to join you this time.

- Tell the students that because they are doing such a great job saying each word as you point to it, you are going to ask some of them to come up to the poem and practice being the teacher. Invite two or three children to come up and take turns pointing below the words as the class reads.

- Because this is likely to be a very popular job, you may want to repeat this lesson on other days. It is wonderful practice both for the children who are doing the pointing (and thus both practicing directionality and internalizing the fact that words are discrete collections of letters) and for the children who are reading along.

From the Classroom: Management Tips—When Anxiety Is Keeping Students from Focusing

While shared reading is designed to engage children on multiple levels and is often a well-loved part of the day, sometimes every class needs some extra assistance staying on task and focused. We notice that this is especially true on days when routines have been changed or when something exciting or anxiety provoking is coming up. As with any other type of lesson, if we aren't on top of management, the most well-planned and well-executed lesson will not reach our students. Following is a snippet of a lesson representing a time during which Andrea had to stop and refocus an unruly class that was thinking much more about an approaching fire drill than it was about shared reading.

Early on in the year in kindergarten, my coteacher and I prepare the children for fire drills. Fire drills tend to provoke anxiety in children new to school, as do changes in daily routines. Putting the fire drill up on the schedule helps the children know what to expect. Later in the year the children will be well prepared for surprise fire drills. Even with planned fire drills, however, there is an element of anxiety involved for many children. This morning the children know that there will be a fire drill right after shared reading time, and Andrea begins to have a feeling that their lack of focus may be related! We enter the lesson as Andrea has called Kevon up to be the teacher and point to the words as the class reads.

"OK, Kevon, let's wait a minute to make sure that everyone's eyes are on your pointer before we start." Kevon and Andrea look out at the children, who are noticeably more wiggly than usual. They wait an extra moment, and finally all children's eyes seem to be on the pointer. "Go ahead," she tells him, and the class starts to read.

"The sun / the sun / the sun / the sun," we read. Andrea notices that the children are not reading together as clearly as they have been. A couple of children are using funny voices as they read.

All of a sudden, a loud, "Stop it, Sonny!" comes from the back row, followed by a fit of giggles from Sonny and then shortly after, from the entire back row. Both Andrea and I have missed whatever has happened and can sense that the class is on the verge of collapsing into laughter over whatever it was. Instead of dealing with the calling out, giggling, and silly voices individually, which would take up a lot of time and probably not get to the root of the issue, Andrea decides to stop the lesson for a talk.

"I'm noticing something, everyone," Andrea says in a serious voice. "Usually when we read together during shared reading, everyone knows just what to do. We read together. We use regular voices. We only say the words in the poem, not any other words. We don't call out. But this morning lots of you seem to be forgetting. I am wondering if maybe instead of thinking about the poem, lots of you are thinking about the fire drill coming up. Sometimes when children are thinking about something and maybe feeling a little nervous about it, it's hard to remember the rules and pay attention to other things. If you were just thinking about the fire drill instead of thinking about shared reading, raise your hand."

Almost all of the hands in the class go up. Whether they all were, in fact, thinking about the fire drill is hard to tell; they may be raising their hands because their friends are. At any rate, it has brought what underlying anxiety may have been occurring to the front of the discussion.

"So here's the thing," Andrea says. "Even if you are thinking a lot about something else, like the fire drill, you still need to follow the rules of shared reading. Kevon is pointing to the words as we read, and you are interrupting his work and your work. When you are thinking about other things during shared reading, you just need to try extra hard to follow our rules. Let's try again, and this time let's remember how strong we've been getting at reading together, using regular voices, saying only the words in the poem, and not any other words."

Whether her hunch that the fire drill was getting in the way was right or not, taking the opportunity to restate the rules of shared reading has an impact on the class. When we resume reading together, the class is cohesive and calm. Andrea makes sure to recognize the children's efforts out loud at the end of shared reading time.

Extending Your Class' Work with "Sun and Moon"

- Divide the class in half. Ask one half to be the readers of the sun stanza and the other group to be the readers of the moon stanza.

- Generating Words with the Same Beginning Sound: You may ask children to think of words that start with the same sound as the letter you've focused your shared reading work on. For example, if you've asked children to identify the letter in the poem that makes the /m/ sound and several individuals have come up and circled (or filled in) the *m*'s, you may then ask them to think of other words that start with that letter. You do not, early in the year, need to write them down in front of the kids. You may want to keep your own record for assessment purposes. If you do choose to write a list of words in front of the kids, you may want to draw their attention to the way the *m* is formed and tuck in a bit more prehandwriting language.

No Nap for Me

Beginning consonants: *m* versus *n* (also *b, g, h, l, s, t, y*)
Sight words: *am, got, how, I, in, me, my, no, not, of, too*

> ### No Nap for Me
> Not me,
> I am not napping.
> Not me,
> I am too big.
> I am busy
> making lots of noise!
> I am busy
> making things!
> Not me,
> I am not napping,
> no matter how you try.
> And no, I am not yawning.
> I've got something in my eye!

Curricular Goals for "No Nap for Me"

Following is a list of possible curricular goals to be accomplished with this poem. You need not spend a lesson on each goal. Devote your lessons to meeting those curricular goals that will best serve your particular class.

- introductory work
- focus on comprehension
- building confidence and community
- focus on directionality
- focus on words as discrete collections of letters
- focus on developing an ear for rhyme
- focus on letter identification, especially *m* versus *n*
- focus on sight words (only if you've begun this work in word study)

Looking for m's and n's: A Lesson Using "No Nap for Me"

Primary Curricular Goals

■ focus on letter identification: *m* versus *n*

Previously Covered

■ introductory work
■ focus on comprehension
■ building confidence and community
■ focus on directionality
■ focus on words as discrete collections of letters
■ focus on developing an ear for rhyme

Setup

■ Before the lesson starts, cover up two of the *m's* and two of the *n's* in the poem with label tape or sticky notes (the *n* in *Not* and the *m* in *me*, and the *m* in *making* and the *n* in *noise*, for example).

■ Gather your students together on the rug or at your class meeting place so that they will all be able to see the words of the poem.

■ Have your pointer available!

Introduction

■ Tell the children to listen carefully as you read the poem through the first time because some of the letters are missing! You will later be asking them to think about what letters are missing and then to come up and write them in.

Interacting with the Text

■ Read the poem through once to your students, exaggerating the missing *n's* and *m's* you've obscured. They will likely think this is hilarious.

■ Ask the students if they noticed the missing letters. Pick one word, such as *me*, say it without the *m*, and ask the students what letter and sound are missing. Do the same for the other words with missing letters as well.

■ Tell the students that sometimes children get confused about the difference between *m* and *n*, because they are a lot alike, and that that is why you are paying attention to those letters in this lesson.

■ Ask students to come up and fill in a missing letter. You may need to support them with an alphabet chart or through modeling writing the letters to help them remember the difference.

Arthur's class has been working with this poem for several days and is now able to read it through with him quite fluently. The class is beginning to become more and more curious about letters and letter sounds, and he decides to take the opportunity to highlight the difference between *m* and *n*. Some children still have difficulty recognizing those two letters visually as well as associating the letters' sounds correctly. Before the lesson began, he covered up the *n* in *Not* and the *m* in *me* as well as the *m* in *making* and the *n* in *noise*. When he read the poem through initially, the class howled with laughter—familiar words sound pretty funny when they are missing a letter! Arthur has helped the students identify that the letters *m* and *n* are the missing ones, and he has invited individuals up to fix the problem. Tonio is the first to approach the poem.

"Tonio, here's the word *me*. Only up here, it just says *–e*! What do you think we need to add in to make *–e* say *me*?"

Tonio thinks a moment and then says, "M?" a little uncertainly.

"Right you are, Tonio. Here's the marker." Arthur hands over a red marker, making it easier for the children to see the letter that Tonio is writing. "Now, add your *m* in right before the *e*. Make sure it's lowercase," he adds, as he sees that Tonio is about to start his letter at the top line.

Tonio adds his *m* and sits down. Arthur asks the class to read the word with him. "Thank goodness you added that *m*, Tonio, or everyone would've been really confused. Now that the *m* is back, the word says *me* instead of *–e*!"

Each time Arthur says the word with the missing letter, the children giggle. He repeats the word and letter and letter sound often so that the children begin to internalize the connection between the letter's sound and its shape. He invites another volunteer to come up and work on adding the *N* in *Not* next, following the same process.

Extending Your Class' Work with "No Nap for Me"

- Ask your students if they can remember a time when they were asked to take a nap, either by a parent or a caregiver or a nursery school teacher, when they had no intention of doing any such thing. What did they do when they were supposed to be napping? Children will have a lot to say about this kind of experience! You may ask them to draw pictures of a time when they didn't want to nap.
- Ask your students to generate a list of things to think about or do to help yourself fall asleep when you don't feel tired.
- As you read the poem, have your students act it out; this can be done simultaneously from their seats on the rug. You may instead ask individuals to act out the poem while the class reads it.

Feeding the Birds

Beginning sounds: *b* versus *d*
Sight words: *an, from, in, love, my, of, our, said, the, they, to*

> ### *Feeding the Birds*
> "Birds love bread,"
> my Grandpa said,
> dropping crumbs
> onto the street.
> In the blink of an eye,
> they rushed from the sky
> to crowd
> around our feet.

Curricular Goals for "Feeding the Birds"

Following is a list of possible curricular goals to be accomplished with this poem. You need not spend a lesson on each goal. Devote your lessons to meeting those curricular goals that will best serve your particular class.

- introductory work
- focus on comprehension
- building confidence and community
- focus on directionality
- focus on words as discrete collections of letters
- focus on developing an ear for rhyme
- focus on letter identification
- focus on sight words (only if you've begun this work in word study)

Focusing on b *versus* d*: A Lesson Using "Feeding the Birds"*

Primary Curricular Goals

- focus on letter identification: *b* versus *d*

Previously Covered

- introductory work
- focus on comprehension
- building confidence and community
- focus on directionality
- focus on words as discrete collections of letters
- focus on developing an ear for rhyme

Setup

- Before the lesson, highlight all of the lowercase *b*'s and *d*'s with transparent colored tape so that they stand out visually to all of the children. In this case, use the same color tape for both *b*'s and *d*'s. (If this is hard to find, you can just use two different-colored markers.)

- Gather your students together on the rug or at your class meeting place so that they will all be able to see the words of the poem.

- It can be useful to have a small chart nearby that reminds children of the difference between *b* and *d*—many teachers use "*b* sees *d*."

- Have your pointer available!

Introduction

- Tell the children to listen carefully as you read the poem through the first time. Tell them you know they will notice that the *b*'s and *d*'s are covered with colored tape and that you will be paying attention to *b*'s and *d*'s later on.

- Invite your students to read with you the second time, making sure to follow your pointer as they read. You may ask them to pay particular attention to the *b*'s and *d*'s as you read those words.

Interacting with the Text

- After reading through the poem together, tell your students that many children confuse lowercase *b*'s and *d*'s and that the poem is going to help the class practice noticing the difference.

- Draw your class' attention to your "*b* sees *d*" chart, reminding them that the *b*'s bump is on the right side of the line and the *d*'s bump is on the left side. Using class landmarks to reinforce left and right is very useful; for example, you may say, "Remember, left is the window side of the classroom, and right is the door side." Have your students practice raising their left and right hands a few times to help them internalize the direction.

- Tell your students that you will be pointing to the lowercase *b*'s and *d*'s in the poem, and that as you point, you'll be asking them to raise their right hands if the letter is a *b* and their left hands if the letter is a *d*.

- As you point to the letters, you may need to remind your students which hand they should raise for which letter. After everyone has raised his hand for a letter (it's likely that students will use each other for support and all end up raising the same hand), have everyone say the name of the letter together before moving on to the next word.

Figure 1–7 *Miles covers b's and d's with red and blue tape.*

From the Classroom: Tips for Supporting English Language Learners

Erin's class makeup does not include a high proportion of English language learners this year—in fact, there is only one child whose first language was not English. Erin has been working to help Joselito connect to other children in the class by assigning him a weekly buddy to help him learn routines and to support him throughout the day. The other children in the class have taken Joselito under their wings, and the buddy job has been a most coveted position! This week, Hans is Joselito's buddy. Erin has asked Hans to sit next to Joselito on the rug and to support him throughout the lesson by whispering directions to him. At this point in the lesson, Erin has explained that she will be pointing to the lowercase *b*'s and *d*'s and will be asking the children to raise their right hands for *b*'s and left hands for *d*'s.

Erin points to the *b* in *bread* and asks, "OK, *b* or *d*, everyone? Remember, right hands (the door side) for *b*, left hands (the window side) for *d*." Many right hands go up immediately. Other children raise their hands more slowly, after looking around the room to see what their classmates are doing. Joselito doesn't raise his hand at all. Hans notices this and reaches over to yank Joselito's right hand up. Joselito pulls away, looking irritated, and then raises his hand himself. Erin is pretty sure that he still doesn't understand exactly what is going on, which is OK at this point—Joselito has been in the country for only a couple of months. She hopes for him to follow along with the class and knows that his understanding will deepen as time goes on. She decides to focus on encouraging Hans to help his buddy in a gentler way.

"Hans, thanks for remembering to look out for Joselito. Remember, though, we want to help Joselito do things on his own in our classroom. You don't have to help him raise his hand by pulling on it—he already knows how to lift his arm up! All you need to do is to show him what to do so that he can do it on his own. Instead of pulling on him, when I point to the next letter, you can tap him on the shoulder so he looks at you, and then point to your own arm to show him that he should raise his. Sound good?"

Hans nods in agreement. Joselito looks relieved; he understands through Erin's facial expressions that she is redirecting Hans, which he appreciates! When Erin points to the next letter (*d* at the end of *bread*), she makes sure to look at Hans. He taps Joselito on the shoulder and then points to his own raised left hand. Joselito's hand shoots up too. Erin smiles at both of them. When all of the left hands are raised, she says, "Let's say this letter and sound together: *d*, /d/. Hans, can you show Joselito? Point to your mouth as you say *d*."

Extending Your Class' Work with "Feeding the Birds"

- Ask your students to generate two lists of words—one list of words beginning with *b* and one list of words beginning with *d*. You may want to hang these two lists near or below a "*b* sees *d*" chart in your room.

- Have your students illustrate the poem. If you are asking students to stretch out words and write the sounds they hear (invented spelling) during writing time, you might ask them to label their pictures; writing the sounds in *bird* and *bread* will give them practice with *b*'s and *d*'s.

Wind

Beginning sounds: *d* versus *w*
Sight words: *about, all, and, be, can, from, if, in, is, it, the, up, will, you, your*

> **Wind**
> Don't worry about the wind.
> It just wants to be heard.
> If you listen very hard,
> you can hear it whisper words:
> "Wake up,
> wake up!
> The wind is here
> to dash over your faces.
> I've rushed all night
> across the land,
> bringing air
> from far-off places."
> Don't worry about the wind.
> Lift the window, let it in.
> Fall asleep and listen hard:
> the wind will tell you
> where it's been!

Curricular Goals for "Wind"

Following is a list of possible curricular goals to be accomplished with this poem. You need not spend a lesson on each goal. Devote your lessons to meeting those curricular goals that will best serve your particular class.

- introductory work
- focus on comprehension
- building confidence and community
- focus on directionality

- focus on words as discrete collections of letters
- focus on developing an ear for rhyme
- focus on letter identification
- focus on sight words (only if you've begun this work in word study)

Focusing on d versus w: A Lesson Using "Wind"

Primary Curricular Goal

- focus on letter identification: *d* versus *w*

Previously Covered

- introductory work
- focus on comprehension
- building confidence and community
- focus on directionality
- focus on words as discrete collections of letters
- focus on developing an ear for rhyme

Setup

- Before the lesson, cover up a few of the *d*'s and *w*'s in the poem with label tape or blank labels.

- Gather your students together on the rug or at your class meeting place so that they will all be able to see the words of the poem.

- Have your pointer available as well as two markers in different colors for children to use when adding in the letters obscured in the poem.

Introduction

- Tell your students that when you read the poem through the first time, they will notice that some sounds are missing from the beginnings of a few of the words. Their job will be to listen carefully as you read, because you will be asking them to come up and add in the missing letters. There is no real need to tell them that you are paying attention to the difference between the /d/ sound and the /w/ sound (many children think that *w* might make the /d/ sound because the name of the letter, "double u," starts with a /d/ sound). Simply paying attention to the two letters and highlighting the sounds they each make will help children distinguish between them.

Interacting with the Text

- Read the poem through, accentuating the words that are missing letters to make it easier for children to hear. Because the children have been working with this poem for several days already, the poem is familiar enough for many of them to recognize missing sounds. They will find the sound of the words with missing letters very funny!

- Reread the first line to the students, omitting the w's: "Don't –orry about the –ind." Ask them to think about what sound is missing from the words. After a student has successfully isolated the /w/ sound, ask another child to say what letter makes that sound.
- Invite a child to come up and add in the w to both words.
- Continue the process, making sure to ask children to use the other color marker when adding the letter d to the poem.
- When all of the missing letters have been added, invite the class to read the poem through with you.

From the Classroom: Tips for Inclusion—Using Visual Cues

Some of the children in K-136, an inclusion classroom, become easily overstimulated when there is extra noise in the room. Rachel in particular is very sensitive to sound, and when other children in the classroom are laughing or talking, she sometimes begins to make a series of high-pitched noises herself. Andrea, the special educator in our classroom, has already had a conversation with the class about helping Rachel "keep the noises inside her head" by not making more sounds or imitating her. She has also created a little picture of a young girl's head, which is taped to the wall directly in front of Rachel's rug spot. In the picture, surrounding the girl's head, there are a few images of noisy things—drums, a trumpet, a person singing—with arrows aiming at the girl's forehead. At the bottom of the picture a line of text says, "I keep the noises inside my head." When Rachel begins making the noises, instead of speaking to her (and thus creating more language for her to sift through), we now just point to the picture, and she is generally able to quiet herself.

Children often find lessons involving missing letters or sounds quite funny; the words sound silly and different, and the class often breaks into peals of laughter when the poem is read for the first time, creating the kind of situation that sometimes leads to Rachel's noises.

"OK, everyone. Listen carefully. There are some letters missing from our poem, and while I read it, your job is to listen carefully and think about what they might be," says Andrea at the beginning of the lesson. She begins to read the poem, starting with the line, "Don't –orry about the –ind." The children, as expected, break into peals of laughter. Rachel (also as expected) begins making a series of high-pitched noises. Andrea catches her eye and points to her sign, which is in arm's reach of the teacher chair in our classroom. Rachel immediately puts her hand to her mouth and smiles. Andrea gives her the OK sign with her fingers and continues reading.

Andrea points to the sign once more toward the end of the poem when the same situation occurs. Before moving on to the section of the lesson in which she'll ask the children to think about what sounds are missing, she congratulates the class on helping Rachel keep the noises inside her head.

"That was so helpful, everyone. You all remembered that when Rachel makes the noises, it's easier for her to push them back in if no other children start making noises—and nobody did! Good for you. And Rachel, you are working so hard on those sounds—good for you, too!

"Now, 'Don't –orry about the –ind?' Hmmmm. What sound do you think is missing there?"

Extending Your Class' Work with "Wind"

■ Write your own class "wind" poem: begin with the phrase "wind can" and ask students to think of things they've seen the wind do. Begin each line with the phrase "wind can," and write the poem in list structure.

■ Ask students to illustrate the shared reading poem or, better yet, your class' own poem.

I Am a Ghost

Sight words: *a, am, can, I, you*

> ### I Am a Ghost
> I can hide.
> I can fly.
> Can I scare you?
> I can try . . .
> BOO!
> —*Melissa Hart*

Curricular Goals for "I Am a Ghost"

Following is a list of possible curricular goals to be accomplished with this poem. You need not spend a lesson on each goal. Devote your lessons to meeting those curricular goals that will best serve your particular class.

- introductory work
- focus on comprehension
- building confidence and community
- focus on directionality
- focus on words as discrete collections of letters
- focus on developing an ear for rhyme
- focus on letter identification
- focus on sight words

Getting to Know Can: A Lesson Using "I Am a Ghost"

Primary Curricular Goals

- focus on sight word: *can*

Previously Covered

- introductory work
- focus on comprehension

- building confidence and community
- focus on directionality
- focus on words as discrete collections of letters
- focus on developing an ear for rhyme
- focus on letter identification

Setup

- Gather your students together on the rug or at your class meeting place so that they will all be able to see the words of the poem.
- Have available colored transparent tape to use for marking the word *can* in the poem.

Introduction

- Tell your students that after you've read the poem through together, you'll be paying special attention to a word that you'll be putting up on the word wall soon, *can*.
- Read the poem once for your students, asking them to follow your pointer with their eyes as you read.

Interacting with the Text

- Read the poem through with your students.

- Tell your students that because you'll be adding *can* to the word wall soon, you want to make sure the word sticks out when they look at the poem. Ask individuals to come up and mark the word each time it appears in the poem.

- Read the poem once through again.

From the Classroom: Dramatizing for Parents

Many schools have monthly morning gatherings when parents are invited into classrooms to read or do other activities with children. Some schools call this event Parents as Learning Partners or something similar. It is October in Melissa's first-grade classroom, and Halloween is pretty much all any of the students are thinking about. Melissa decides to launch this month's Parents as Learning Partners event with a recitation of the poem her class has been studying, "I Am a Ghost." The parents are stationed near the work tables, and all of the kids are gathered together on the rug facing them. They have practiced reciting the poem together many times, so they belt it out with confidence. When they come to the end and say, "BOO!" all of the first graders leave the rug and rush over to their parents, putting on their best scary ghost faces! After the hilarity has calmed, Melissa calls the kids back to the rug and launches the rest of the morning's activities.

Pretend

Beginning sounds: *b, f, j, l, p, q, w, y*
Ending sounds: *d f, n*
Sight words: *a, am, I*

> *Pretend*
> I am a wild pirate.
> I am a fairy queen.
> I am a falling yellow leaf.
> I am a jumping bean!

Curricular Goals for "Pretend"

Following is a list of possible curricular goals to be accomplished with this poem. You need not spend a lesson on each goal. Devote your lessons to meeting those curricular goals that will best serve your particular class.

- introductory work
- focus on comprehension
- building confidence and community
- focus on directionality
- focus on words as discrete collections of letters
- focus on developing an ear for rhyme
- focus on letter identification
- focus on new sight words (only if you've begun this work in word study)

Missing Am: A Lesson Using "Pretend"

Primary Curricular Goals

- focus on sight word: *am*

Previously Covered

- introductory work
- focus on comprehension
- building confidence and community

- focus on directionality
- focus on words as discrete collections of letters
- focus on developing an ear for rhyme
- focus on letter identification

Setup

- Before the lesson, cover up the word *am* every time it occurs in the poem with label tape or blank labels.
- Gather your students together on the rug or at your class meeting place so that they will all be able to see the words of the poem.
- Have your pointer available, as well a marker in a different color from the color in which the poem is written.

Introduction

- Tell your students that when you read the poem through the first time, they will notice that a whole word is missing from each line. Because the poem is familiar to them, most children will easily be able to remember (or use context to figure out) that the word is *am*.

Interacting with the Text

- Read the poem through, accentuating the missing word to make it easier for children to hear.

- Ask children to guess what word is missing. You may ask them to whisper the word they think is missing in a neighbor's ear. Ask one child to share the missing word.

- Show the children how to write the word *am*. You may write on a nearby chalkboard or dry-erase board, or even on the same chart as the poem. Ask children to pay attention to how you form the letters as well, and have the class spell the word with you when you are finished.

- Invite individual children to come up one at a time and add in the missing words in the poem. You may need to remind them to use your example as a reference point.

- When all of the missing words have been added, invite the class to read the poem through with you.

From the Classroom: Tucking in Handwriting Tips

Any time you are writing in front of your class, you have an opportunity to reinforce skills that children will use when they begin handwriting instruction, if they haven't already. Even if you do not formally teach handwriting in your classroom, you can use the writing you do in front of students to help introduce writing letters in the way that you hope for them to continue writing letters on their own. In the previous lesson, the word *am* was left out of the poem, providing children with opportunities to fill it in. Not only are you able to introduce sight words in this manner, but you are also able to show children how the letters are written.

Many kindergartners seem to naturally start writing letters at the bottom line rather than at the top. Bob takes the opportunity to reinforce starting at the top of the letter as he shows his class how to write the word *am*. He carries on a sort of monologue as he writes the letters. Interestingly enough, this kind of monologue is often fascinating to kids, and his class is riveted.

That's right, Jacob. The missing word is *am*. If you were also thinking that *am* was the missing word, raise two thumbs.

"Look, Jacob; everyone agrees with you! OK. Let me show you how we write the word *am*. We'll write it in lowercase letters here, because it's in lowercase letters in the poem.

"I'll start with the *a*. When we write a lowercase *a*, everyone, we start at the middle line, the dotted one. We circle down and then back up to where we started. But wait, we're not done! Trace the line back down again, and give your *a* a little tail. There we go.

"Now for the *m*. It's also lowercase, so where should I start, everyone?"

"The middle!"

"OK, I'll start at the middle line. Straight down to the bottom, then back up the same line. One bump, back up, and another bump. I'll end here on the bottom line. There it is. The word *am*—*a, m*. Let's spell it together."

"*A, m, am*," spells the class.

"OK, who'd like to come up and add one of our missing *ams* to the poem? Don't forget to start at the middle line!"

If you are using a particular handwriting program, the language you use when modeling writing for children should match the language that you use when following the handwriting program.

Extending Your Class' Work with "Pretend"

- This is a good poem to act out because it is all about pretending! You may have the entire class act out the poem as you read it. You may have small groups of four act it out as the rest of the class reads. You may divide the whole class in four and have each section act out one of the roles described in the poem.
- Extend the poem with your class: Below the poem, write the phrase "I am," and then ask students to think about the things that they become when they are pretending. There is no need to continue the rhyme scheme of the poem. You may choose to ask students to share the pen and write in the words "I am" themselves as you add each new line.

■ Create a booklet of poems the class has studied printed in large font for children to read during independent reading time. Even though a poem's level may be beyond the typical independent level of your students, their familiarity with the poems from shared reading time will support them, as will picture cues. (See Figure 1–8.)

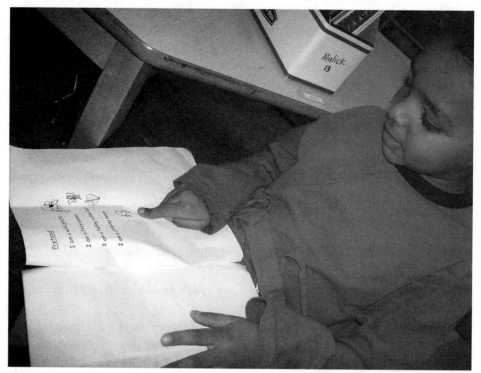

Figure I–8 *Malick reads shared reading poems during readers workshop.*

We Will Go

Beginning and ending letter sounds: *b, f, g, n, r, s, t, w*
Sight words: *by, for, go, in, the, us, we, will*

> ### We Will Go
> We will go by bike.
> We will go by train.
> We will go by taxi.
> We will go in the rain.
>
> We will go by foot.
> We will go by bus.
> We will go in the sunshine.
> The circus waits for us!

Curricular Goals for "We Will Go"

Following is a list of possible curricular goals to be accomplished with this poem. You need not spend a lesson on each goal. Devote your lessons to meeting those curricular goals that will best serve your particular class.

- introductory work
- focus on comprehension
- building confidence and community
- focus on directionality
- focus on words as discrete collections of letters
- focus on developing an ear for rhyme
- focus on letter identification
- focus on sight words

Finding Sight Words: A Lesson Using "We Will Go"

Primary Curricular Goal

- focus on new sight words

Previously Covered

- ▨ introductory work
- ▨ focus on comprehension
- ▨ building confidence and community
- ▨ focus on directionality
- ▨ focus on words as discrete collections of letters
- ▨ focus on developing an ear for rhyme
- ▨ focus on letter identification

Setup

- ▨ Before this lesson, you should have added the words *we*, *will*, and *go* to your word wall (or these words should be familiar to your students).

- ▨ Gather your students together on the rug or at your class meeting place so that they will all be able to see the words of the poem.

- ▨ Have your pointer available as well as several different colors of transparent tape, cut into rectangles that will fit over the sight words in the poem.

Introduction

- ▨ Tell your students that after they read through the poem once, they will be looking for words they recognize from the class word wall.

Interacting with the Text

- ▨ Read the poem once through together (your students will probably be able to read along with you, if they have had several opportunities to learn the poem previously).

- ▨ Ask your students if they recognize any of the words in the poem as being the same as words on your class word wall. Call on individuals to say out loud a word that they recognize. (Clearly the students' responses will vary from class to class!)

- ▨ Tell your class that you will be asking three children to come up and put some colored tape over a sight word so that the words will be easier to see in the poem. It is likely that the students will recognize the words *we*, *will*, and *go* first.

- ▨ Invite one child to the front of the room after hearing which word the child would like to highlight. Have available enough transparent tape rectangles to cover each instance of the word. Ask the child first to point to and then cover up the word each time she sees it. Invite the next two children up and follow the same routine, but make sure that each sight word is covered with a different color tape; for example, all of the *wes* may be yellow, all of the *wills* may be blue, and all of the *gos* may be green.

- ▨ Read the poem once through again as a class.

From the Classroom: Management Tips

Sometimes the most thoroughly and appropriately planned lessons don't go exactly the way we imagine them. We may have unpredicted interruptions. We may find that we've missed the mark a bit and have planned too much. We may find that our students breeze through an activity quickly and that we could actually keep going.

In this example, Sally discovers that her students are not recognizing the sight words in the poem as readily as she had imagined and that it is taking more time for them to locate and cover each word with tape than she anticipated. As a result, the children have been spending more time waiting on the rug than she hoped, making them antsy. Her student Charlie has just finished covering up all of the *wes* in the poem, and Sally calls on the next child, Steven, to come cover the word he noticed, *will*, with tape.

Steven comes up to the front of the room and Sally hands him the first rectangle of blue tape.

"OK, Stevie, where do you see the word *will* in our poem?"

Steven ponders the poem carefully. As he is looking, Sally looks out over the kids on the rug. They are not chatting or giggling, but there seems to be a bit of extra motion happening. Sally senses them becoming restless as Steven looks for the word *will*. Theo is shaking his head from side to side and, Sally imagines, paying more attention to the feel of his hair swishing around than he is to the poem. A Velcro sneaker is unfastened here, some corduroy pants are rubbed together there.

Steven finds the *will*. Sally thanks him and hands him another piece of tape. He finds the next two instances of the word more quickly, but the children on the rug are clearly losing focus. Sally considers moving forward after Steven sits down, even though she had planned for a child to come and cover up the word *go* as well. She looks out at the sea of gently wiggling, fidgeting, head-shaking bodies and realizes that it may be time to move on to center time; she can always come back to the poem during a transition later in the day.

"K-144, I know I told you that we were going to cover up three words today, but I am thinking that you have been sitting on the rug for a long time now and that you have been working very hard to stay still and to think about the words in the poem. I am thinking that we will find some time to cover up the next word wall word later in the day, because it looks to me that this is a class of kindergartners who are ready for center time. Put two thumbs up if you are ready to get started."

Extending Your Class' Work with "We Will Go"

■ This is a poem that children will be able to read independently without a lot of practice, especially if they are familiar with the three repeating words *we*, *will*, and *go*.

■ You may ask individuals to stand up and recite the poem for the class if they are comfortable doing so.

■ You might create a collection of poems that your class has been studying during shared reading time for the children to read during independent reading time.

■ You could post the "We Will Go" chart in the room somewhere that is accessible to the children so that they might practice reading it during center time.

Sam's Map

Beginning and ending letter sounds: *b, c, f, h, l, m, n, r, s, t, w, z*
Spelling patterns: *am, ap, at* (short *a*)
Sight words: *a, and, at, friend, he, his, my, the, with*

> ### Sam's Map
> My friend Sam
> loves his subway map.
> He's happy that he has one.
> He looks at his map
> before his nap.
> He looks at his map
> with his family.
> He rests his map upon his lap
> and imagines the trains underground:
> zooming around with a wham and a slam
> past rats and bats
> and little lost cats.
> Sam loves his subway map!

Curricular Goals for "Sam's Map"

Following is a list of possible curricular goals to be accomplished with this poem. You need not spend a lesson on each goal. Devote your lessons to meeting those curricular goals that will best serve your particular class.

- introductory work
- focus on comprehension
- building confidence and community
- focus on directionality
- focus on words as discrete collections of letters
- focus on developing an ear for rhyme
- focus on letter identification

- focus on spelling patterns
- focus on sight words

Noticing and Charting Words with Short a: A Lesson Using "Sam's Map"

Primary Curricular Goals

- focus on letter identification: short *a*

Previously Covered

- introductory work
- focus on comprehension
- building confidence and community
- focus on directionality
- focus on words as discrete collections of letters
- focus on developing an ear for rhyme

Setup

- Gather your students together on the rug or at your class meeting place so that they will all be able to see the words of the poem.
- Have your pointer available as well as markers and a separate piece of chart paper (or board space) to use for charting the short *a* words in the poem.

Introduction

- Tell your students that after reading the poem through once together, you will be spying out words in the poem that contain the short *a* sound and then collecting them on a separate piece of paper.

Interacting with the Text

- Read the poem once through together (your students will probably be able to read along with you, if they have had several opportunities to learn the poem previously).

- Tell your students that today instead of just noticing and pointing out words with the short *a* sound in the poem, you'll be making a list together of all of the short *a* words they can see. Have your charting paper available.

- Model noticing a word with short *a* in the poem—*map*, for example. Point to the word and have your students say it with you so that they have the short *a* sound in their ears. Write the word *map* on your chart. You may want to model another word for them if you feel they need another example.

- Ask your students to raise their hands if they can see other words that have the short *a* sound in them. Call on individuals to come up to the poem and point out the word they've noticed and then add that word to the chart paper.

■ Continue until your students have found and charted all of the short *a* words or until their attention is waning!

■ If your class is ready, you may want to categorize the words on your chart according to spelling pattern—all the *ap* words together and so on.

From the Classroom: Managing Word Charting

Students have had several experiences with "Sam's Map" before Harry presents this lesson. Most of his end-of-the-year kindergartners are able to say most of the poem's words with him as they read together. Harry's class has already spent time listening for rhyming words in the poem, which directly prepared them for this lesson, as the rhyming words all feature the short *a* sound. Noticing rhyme is often an easier and more automatic task than isolating a particular letter sound. Today, Harry and his class will make a chart of the short *a* words in the poem. Because his students are still becoming comfortable with vowel recognition, Harry chooses not to categorize the words by spelling pattern, but to simply collect a list of all the short *a* words in the poem. He will, however, distinguish between words with the short and the long *a* sounds.

"OK, everyone. Today, since we've been getting lots of practice noticing words with the /a/ sound, we're going to make a chart together of all of the /a/ words we can find in 'Sam's Map.' I'll show you what I mean.

"First, I'm going to see if I can find a word that has the /a/ sound. . . . Aha! *Map.* Does that work, everyone?" The class agrees. Harry uncaps his marker and writes the word *map* at the top of a piece of construction paper he's hung up near the easel.

"Can anyone see another *a* word I should add to our chart? Quiet hands, please. Sarita?"

"*Sam* has an *a*."

"Yep, it sure does. I'll just write that down here next to *map.* Now it's going to be your turn, guys, to add the words to the chart. Does anyone else see a word with *a* in it? Marcus, what do you see?"

"I see the one with the *n*," Marcus says.

"Come on up and point to the word you mean, Marcus." The boy points to the word *nap.* "You're right, Marcus—that word does have the /a/ sound in it. Any guesses about how we say that word?"

Marcus is not yet ready to recognize words out of context, and Harry can see by his puzzled face that he is not sure what word he's found.

"Shall we ask the kids for some ideas, Marcus?" asks Harry. Marcus nods an affirmative, and hands shoot up.

"Go ahead, Tamar."

"That's *nap*!" bellows Tamar.

"Sound right, Marcus?" Harry asks. When Marcus nods, Harry hands him the marker and asks him to write the word *nap* on the chart paper below the word *map*.

Marcus carefully writes the letters.

Harry calls on several more students to point out and record *a* words on the list. When Alice enthusiastically points out the word *day*, Harry says, "You are quite right that the word *day* has an *a* in it, Alice, but it makes a different sound than it makes in the words on our chart. Vowels are tricky that way; they sometimes sound different, depending on which letters they have for neighbors! In the word *day*, the *a* goes 'aaaaay.' In the other words on our chart, it goes 'a.' Let me give you another color of marker, and you can write your word down here in another section so we can start keeping track of the different sounds *a* can make."

Extending Your Class' Work with "Sam's Map"

- If you live in an area that doesn't use public transportation, your students will probably be unfamiliar with the subway. You may choose to weave this poem into a class study of transportation, which is a popular study in many early-childhood classrooms. You may want to obtain a subway map and photographs of the subway to give your students some background information.

- Living and teaching in New York City, I have certain students every year who are absolutely enamored with the subway system. If you are lucky enough to have one of these young subway experts in the class, you may want to have that student bring in a map and talk to the class about his favorite subway lines.

Bored

Beginning and ending letter sounds: *b, c, d, f, g, l, p, s, t*
Spelling patterns: *og, op, ot* (short *o*)
Sight words: *a, at, his, in, on, the, with*

> **Bored**
> The dog
> with the dot
> on the top
> of his nose
> sat on a log
> in the fog,
> just barking
> at crows.

Curricular Goals for "Bored"

Following is a list of possible curricular goals to be accomplished with this poem. You need not spend a lesson on each goal. Devote your lessons to meeting those curricular goals that will best serve your particular class.

- introductory work
- focus on comprehension
- building confidence and community
- focus on directionality
- focus on words as discrete collections of letters
- focus on developing an ear for rhyme
- focus on letter identification, especially short *o*
- focus on spelling patterns
- focus on sight words

Generating Words That End Like Dog: A Lesson Using "Bored"

Primary Curricular Goals

- ▦ focus on letter identification: short *o*
- ▦ focus on spelling pattern: *og*

Previously Covered

- ▦ introductory work
- ▦ focus on comprehension
- ▦ building confidence and community
- ▦ focus on directionality
- ▦ focus on words as discrete collections of letters
- ▦ focus on developing an ear for rhyme

Setup

- ▦ In a previous lesson, you will have asked children to listen for and locate words that end in *og*. They will have highlighted those words with transparent colored tape.

- ▦ Gather your students together on the rug or at your class meeting place so that they will all be able to see the words of the poem.

- ▦ Have your pointer available as well as a marker and an extra piece of chart paper or space on the poem chart to write a list of words.

Introduction

- ▦ Tell your students that after you read the poem through once, they will read along with you. Tell them that because they know the poem well by now, they will be paying special attention to words that end in *og*, like the word *dog*.

Interacting with the Text

- ▦ Read the poem through once on your own, asking your students to be listeners. Even though many children would be able to read along with you the first time, it doesn't hurt to help them get the sound of the poem in their heads before asking them to join in.

- ▦ Ask the children to read along with you, paying special attention to the words that end in *og* like *dog*. You may remind them that those words have been highlighted already with a particular color of tape.

- ▦ Ask children if they can think of any other words that end in *og* like *dog*.

- ▦ Write a list of the words that your students generate either on a separate piece of paper that you can post in the room or on the same chart paper containing the poem.

When asking your students to generate words, it is a given that not all of their suggestions will fit in with the pattern you suggest. Sometimes this is because there is another spelling pattern that sounds the same. Sometimes it is because children are not hearing the pattern as a whole and are focusing on only one part of it. Sometimes children are still developing an ear for rhyme and may answer with a word related by meaning rather than by structure. It is important to respect each child's offering, whether it fits with your pattern or not—in fact, mistakes often provide opportunities for additional teaching. As K-136 works on generating words that end in *og* like the word *dog*, I try to acknowledge each child's effort while clarifying the teaching point for the class as a whole.

"OK, everyone, so can you think of some more words that end in *og*, like the word *dog* in our poem? You can say the words you are thinking quietly to yourself for a few seconds to help yourselves think."

"*Log!*" says Kenny when I call on him, followed shortly after by Tino's suggestion, *fog*. Often, if a poem contains other examples of the pattern in question, students will notice these first; that's not a problem, and in fact they are being quite resourceful to use the text around them for suggestions. I write the two words under the heading "*og* Words" below the poem.

I call on Stephan, who has recently become more and more of a participant in our shared reading activities. I am pleased to see that he is raising his hand.

"*Puppy!*" he says, beaming. When a couple of students giggle, I ask for their silence with a raised palm and a quick serious look.

"Actually, Stephan, I think I know what you were thinking there. Were you thinking about a word that *means* the same thing as the word *dog?*"

"Yeah," says Stephan, looking a bit uncertain.

"Aha," I say. "So we'll write your word over here, on the other side of the paper. Stephan was thinking of a word that means the same thing, everyone, so that word doesn't go on our list of words that *sound* the same because they end in *og*. But we can put it over here. Stephan, you be thinking of words that *sound* the same as *dog*, like *log* and *fog* do. I'll come back to you, OK?" He nods, thinking. I move on.

After adding Sylvie's suggestion, *frog*, and Luciano's, *smog*, I call on Peter.

"How about *dot* and *cot?*" he asks.

"Let's check with the class, Peter. *Dot* and *cot*. Do those sound just like *dog* and *fog* and *log?*"

"No," several students say. I know that our class has built up enough of a sense of trust and collaboration that Peter will not feel embarrassed by this interaction. He knows that we are working on solving a problem together.

"They sound pretty similar, though, Peter. All of those words have the short *o* sound in them, and I can see that you are learning to hear short *o*! We can start a new list here, words that end in *ot*, like Peter's words *dot* and *cot*. Let's get back to our *og* words, but Peter, we can add some more *ot* words to your list later, OK?"

Extending Your Class' Work with "Bored"

■ Ask your students to act out the poem as you read it. You'll have to set some guidelines about barking first!

■ Ask your students to illustrate the poem. You may want to have a discussion first about how they will include all of the poem's details in their drawings or even to model drawing for them. The poem is full of specific directional words—the dot is on top of the dog's nose, the dog is on top of the log. This may be hard for some students to visualize, and you may need to model for them before they attempt drawing on their own.

Wren

Beginning and ending letter sounds: *b, c, f, h, j, m, p, s, t, w*
Spelling patterns: *eg, en, et* (short e)
Blend: *wr*
Sight words: *a, and, be, can, for, get, her, in, like, me, my, off, on, said, the, took, you*

> **Wren**
> Wren perched on a peg
> with little wren legs
> and looked me in the eye.
> I said, "I'll get my net.
> You can be my pet.
> I just bet
> you can teach me how to fly!"
> Wren stretched her wings
> and shook her head
> and took off like a jet
> for the sky.

Curricular Goals for "Wren"

Following is a list of possible curricular goals to be accomplished with this poem. You need not spend a lesson on each goal. Devote your lessons to meeting those curricular goals that will best serve your particular class.

- introductory work
- focus on comprehension
- building confidence and community
- focus on directionality
- focus on words as discrete collections of letters
- focus on developing an ear for rhyme
- focus on letter identification

- focus on spelling patterns
- focus on sight words

Generating *et* Words: A Lesson Using "Wren"

Primary Curricular Goals

- focus on spelling pattern: *et*

Previously Covered

- introductory work
- focus on comprehension
- building confidence and community
- focus on directionality
- focus on words as discrete collections of letters
- focus on developing an ear for rhyme
- focus on letter identification

Setup

- Gather your students together on the rug or at your class meeting place so that they will all be able to see the words of the poem.
- Have your pointer available as well as either an extra piece of chart paper or some space on the board for writing.

Introduction

- Tell your students that after you read through the poem together, you will be paying attention to all of the words that end in *et*, like *wet*, and that you will be making a list of those words together.

Interacting with the Text

- Read through the poem once with your students. Because they will have had several experiences with the poem already, most of the students will be saying most of the words of the poem with you.

- Remind your students that you will be paying attention to the words that end in *et*. Ask two or three children to come up to the poem (one at a time) and point to a word that ends in *et*.

- Tell your students that you will be making a list together of all of the other words they can think of that end in *et*. Begin the list by writing down the words that students have identified in the poem. You may choose to write the *et* ending in a different color or to underline it so that it is more visible to the children.

- Ask individuals to say other words that end the same way. Write them on your chart. Continue until your time for shared reading is up.

■ Read through the chart together, and post it in the room. You can remind students (if appropriate for your class) that they can use the chart to help them when they are writing words.

From the Classroom: A Conversation to Deepen Comprehension

Because shared reading is such a wonderful way to work on letter-sound identification, sight words, spelling patterns, and other skills, it can be easy to focus more attention on those things than on the poem's meaning. Because the poems that are useful for this kind of work are often by nature quite short and simple, there may not be a whole lot of unpacking to do in terms of discussing the poem's meaning with your class. Conversations about meaning, however, complete the picture for children and help keep shared reading feeling like an authentic literary experience instead of simply a time for word work. The following is a conversation that Elena facilitates with her kindergartners about the poem "Wren."

"So, everyone, we've been working on getting to know our new poem, 'Wren.' Something happens at the end of the poem that I have been getting more and more curious about and I wonder if you are curious, too. At the end of the poem, the little wren 'takes off like a jet for the sky.' First of all, what's going on there? What's happening? Jared?"

"The bird is just flying away from him."

"Do you suppose he's flying fast or slow, Jared?"

"I think fast, like a jet!"

"Thumbs up if you were thinking that the wren is flying away really fast at the end of the poem," says Elena, and most of the children raise two thumbs. "Looks like most of you agree about that. Well here's my second question. Why do you suppose the wren takes off so fast all of a sudden? Quiet hands . . . Ari?"

"He doesn't want to get stuck in the net! He just wants to go away and not be a pet!" Ari says.

"Carla, do you have more to say about that?"

"Yeah, that little kid wants to catch him and make him a pet and keep him in a cage and then he can't be with his family. So he goes fast away."

The conversation continues for a few more moments, with children sharing ideas about the wren's flight. Elena is satisfied that her students understand the poem.

Picnic

Beginning and ending letter sounds: *b, c, f, h, j, m, p, s, t, w*
Spelling patterns: *ug, un, ut* (short *u*)
Sight words: *a, has, in, is, much, so, the, up, we*

> *Picnic*
> A slug has slunk
> up the side of Dad's mug.
> Three bugs jumped in
> the water jug.
> Six yummy plums
> warm up in the sun.
> We eat.
> We run.
> We doze.
> We hum.
> Eating outside
> is so much fun!

Curricular Goals for "Picnic"

Following is a list of possible curricular goals to be accomplished with this poem. You need not spend a lesson on each goal. Devote your lessons to meeting those curricular goals that will best serve your particular class.

- introductory work
- focus on comprehension
- building confidence and community
- focus on directionality
- focus on words as discrete collections of letters
- focus on developing an ear for rhyme
- focus on letter identification, especially short *u*
- focus on spelling patterns
- focus on sight words

Primary Curricular Goals

- ■ focus on comprehension

Previously Covered

- ■ introductory work

Setup

- ■ You will want to have introduced the poem to your students so that they'll have heard it before on at least one previous occasion, but this lesson can take place at any point along the way.

- ■ Gather your students together on the rug or at your class meeting place so that they will all be able to see the words of the poem.

Introduction

- ■ Tell your students that after you read the poem through once, they will read along with you. Tell them that you will then be teaching them some gestures to do as they read the poem so that their bodies will show what is happening.

Interacting with the Text

- ■ After your read the poem together once, demonstrate a gesture for each action in the poem—any clear, simple, illustrative motion that children can do while sitting together on the rug should work (miming a slug with one finger wiggling up the side of the other hand, miming the sun coming out, etc.).

- ■ Read the poem through together again, this time encouraging children to follow along with you as you accompany your reading with gestures.

- ■ Repeat a couple of times until all of the children are following along.

From the Classroom: Tips for Supporting English Language Learners—Using Props

Even though we have been using some gestures to accompany our reading of the poem "Picnic" in an effort to support the children's comprehension (and to engage them physically), I sense that Peter, who has recently joined our class from Germany, could use a bit more support. Because this is a poem that lends itself easily to acting out, I've collected some props to use as we read so that I can literally show Peter what is happening in the poem. I've made a simple slug out of paper. I grabbed the mug I keep in the room for my morning tea. I pulled three little plastic bugs out of the animals we keep in the block center. I grabbed a plastic container (jug) that we use for holding water in the painting center. I also pulled an old tablecloth out of the pretend center to lay down on the rug. I picked up some plums at the bodega on the corner on my way to school (pictures work just fine, too). This morning I have the kids sit in a circle instead of in their regular rug spots so that I can lay out our picnic blanket in the center of the circle.

"OK, everyone. We are sitting in a different way today because I want you all to be able to see the things I brought to help us act out our poem as we read it." I show the kids all of the objects I've collected and draw their attention to each place in the poem where the props will be used. I tell them that I will use the props the first time around, but that children will have a chance to try them out as well. I spread the tablecloth out like a picnic blanket.

We read the line "A slug has slunk / up the side of Dad's mug," and I have the little paper slug crawl up my coffee mug. The kids giggle at my look of mock horror.

We read "Three bugs jumped in / the water jug," and I toss the little plastic bugs in the jug one by one.

We read, "Six yummy plums / warm up in the sun," and I line up the plums one by one.

As we read "We eat. / We run. / We doze. / We hum," I model the gestures we've been using as we read, and the kids spontaneously join in. As we read the last lines of the poem, we all raise our hands as if we're cheering.

I notice that Peter has been watching carefully as I've used the props. It is hard to tell how much he comprehends, but he definitely seems more engaged than he has in the past—as do many of the other children who are native English speakers! We read the poem once more through and I model using the props. The next time around, I'll ask Peter and some other children to come up and sit around the blanket and use the props.

This is likely to be a pretty popular activity, so you may want to schedule in more than one session's worth.

Extending Your Class' Work with "Picnic"

- Have the props available with a copy of the poem for kids to act out on their own during center time. You may need to model for them first.

- Ask them to think about what foods they would take with them on a picnic and then have them draw or write about those foods.

Backyard Digging

Beginning and ending letter sounds: *b, c, d, g, h, l, g, m, n, p*
Spelling patterns: *ig, ip* (short *i*)
Sight words: *a, is, my, or*

> ### Backyard Digging
>
> Dig, dig, dig.
> My hole is getting big!
> My shovel tip
> hit a buried ship,
> or a coin,
> or a bone,
> or a mummy's hip!
> Dig, dig, dig.
> My hole is getting big!

Curricular Goals for "Backyard Digging"

Following is a list of possible curricular goals to be accomplished with this poem. You need not spend a lesson on each goal. Devote your lessons to meeting those curricular goals that will best serve your particular class.

- introductory work
- focus on comprehension
- building confidence and community
- focus on directionality
- focus on words as discrete collections of letters
- focus on developing an ear for rhyme
- focus on letter identification
- focus on spelling patterns
- focus on sight words

Figure 1–9   *Sylvie points below the words in "Backyard Digging" as K-136 reads along.*

Noticing *ip* and *ig*: A Lesson Using "Backyard Digging"

Primary Curricular Goals

- focus on spelling patterns: *ip, ig*

Previously Covered

- introductory work
- focus on comprehension
- building confidence and community
- focus on directionality
- focus on words as discrete collections of letters
- focus on developing an ear for rhyme
- focus on letter identification

Setup

- Gather your students together on the rug or at your class meeting place so that they will all be able to see the words of the poem.
- Have your pointer available as well as some appropriately sized rectangles of transparent tape in two different colors.

Introduction

- Tell your students that after you read the poem through once together, you will be searching for words that end in *ig*, like *dig*, and words that end in *ip*, like *hip*.

Interacting with the Text

- After your read the poem together once, tell children that they will be searching for words in the poem that end in *ig* or *ip*. If you are studying these spelling patterns in word study, it is helpful to draw the children's attention to that work so that they can keep it in mind as they study the poem.

- Start with words that end in *ig*. Model looking and listening for a word that ends with *ig* in the poem and then covering up just the *ig* with a piece of precut transparent colored tape.

- Ask students to raise a hand if they see another word that ends this way, and invite individuals up to the poem to first point to the word and then cover the *ig* ending with a piece of transparent tape.

- If it feels appropriate for your class, when the *ig* words have been marked, you may ask children to hunt for *ip* words as well, or you may choose to save this activity for the next shared reading session.

- Read the poem through again together when you have finished marking the words.

From the Classroom: Tips for Inclusion— the Physically Impulsive Child

Adam is a little boy in our class who has been diagnosed with attention deficit disorder (ADD). His issues with attention manifest in a variety of ways in our classroom. Sitting with the other children on the rug without calling out, touching other children, or moving away from his spot is a particular challenge for Adam. Early in the year, Andrea and I changed Adam's rug spot to the front row, right in front of the teacher chair. This helped a bit, as we were able to whisper reminders to him without speaking out loud across the rest of the class. However, Adam continued to have difficulty staying still in his rug spot and would often flop over, stick his legs out in front of him, turn around to touch his neighbors, or even crawl away from his rug spot to touch a nearby book. Sometimes something so small as a piece of fluff on the rug would catch his attention and he would leave his rug spot to go inspect it. We found that we were giving Adam verbal reminders quite often and that these reminders did not seem to be helping Adam internalize the expectations for sitting on the rug.

Andrea decided to try a visual cue instead; her hypothesis was that not only would a visual reminder cut out all of the verbal reminders, which were clearly interrupting lessons, but it might clarify expectations for Adam. Andrea drew on tagboard a picture of a little boy sitting with his legs crossed and his hands in his lap (a photograph would work just as well) and posted this on the wall in front of Adam's rug spot. In the snippet of a shared reading lesson that follows, she is making use of the sign to remind Adam of rug expectations. The children are just getting to know the poem and are practicing reading it together.

"All right, everyone," says Andrea, "let's try reading together this time. Follow the pointer as I read and try to match your voice to my voice."

As the class begins to read together, Adam is focused on the pointer for perhaps the first line of text, and then something else catches his attention. A little piece of shiny paper has fallen off a collage that is hanging above the rug and is lying under the teacher chair. As the class continues to read, Adam crawls away from his rug spot and reaches under the teacher chair. Without stopping the reading, Andrea taps Adam on the shoulder with her free hand. When he looks up, she taps audibly on his sign. He quickly corrects himself, and she gives him the OK sign with her free hand. He grins and looks back to the chart paper.

After another line, Adam turns around in his spot because as Alia, who is sitting behind him, enthusiastically belts out the poem, she leans forward and gently touches his back. Adam stops reading to attempt a conversation with Alia. Andrea taps him and touches the sign again. He corrects himself and reads through the final lines with the rest of the class.

When the class has finished the poem, Andrea says, "Adam, you are really letting that sign work for you. Both times I pointed to it, you corrected yourself right away. We didn't have to stop reading—you knew just what to do. Good for you! OK, everyone, let's read through it once more before snack time."

Extending Your Class' Work with "Backyard Digging"

- Ask your students to imagine what might be buried in their own backyards (or in the dirt at the park in their neighborhoods, if they don't have a yard). Discuss their ideas, and then have them draw or write.

- If you have any nonfiction books about archaeology with good illustrations or photographs of people digging up dinosaur bones and so on, it can be fun to show those illustrations to children after reading the poem.

CHAPTER TWO

Moving Forward

Children moving into this next phase of shared reading are still delighted by the sound and look of words. They will have developed an understanding that words are made up of letters, and they will have a stronger grasp on letters and letter sounds. While vowels continue to be confusing, children in this phase first begin to sort out the short-vowel sounds in CVC words and later are able to see and remember long vowels created by adding a silent *e* as well. Children will become comfortable identifying and using digraphs and two-letter consonant blends as well. The poems also provide examples of the simple word endings *s* and *ing*. While children are more able to notice, identify, and use more sophisticated spelling patterns and sight words, they are absolutely still interested in playing with poems—acting them out, illustrating them, reading them over to each other. All of those activities help develop fluency and phrasing. Children at this stage are now more able to understand figurative language, which opens up whole new venues of class conversation!

■ Sight Words Appearing in This Chapter's Poems

a, all, am, an, and, are, as, at, before, but, by, could, did, do, down, ever, fine, for, from, go, going, have, he, her, him, his, I, in, into, is, it, how, just, like, look, me, most, my, nice, not, now, of, off, on, one, or, our, saw, see, she, so, some, than, that, the, them, then, they, this, to, too, took, up, us, was, we, what, when, where, which, while, who, why, will, with, you

■ Spelling Patterns Appearing in This Chapter's Poems

Spelling patterns: *all, ell, ill; ang, ing, ong, ung; ank, ink, onk, unk*
Digraphs: *ch, sh, th, wh*
Blends: *sk, sm, sp, st; fl, pl, sl, vl; dr, fr, pr, tr*
Endings: *ing, s*
Long vowels: *a–e, i–e, o–e, u–e*

■ Mining Poems for Teaching Points: Curricular Goals Associated with Continuing Shared Reading Work

While the curricular goals are introduced in a sequence that many teachers might choose to follow, the sequence is certainly not set in stone. You might choose to focus on sight words before focusing on spelling patterns, for example, or you might choose not to spend time on sight words at all from a particular poem. You also might focus a couple of lessons on the same curricular goal, especially if your students seem to need more time.

Introductory Work

Children entering the next phase of shared reading are moving beyond the pre-reading stage into being readers themselves. Children typically have a small bank of simple sight words at their disposal and strong phonemic awareness. They have internalized the directionality of reading and understand that words are made up of discrete collections of letters. They are ready to look not just at beginning and ending sounds but at parts of words. They can recognize and learn new simple spelling patterns. Reading with fluency and expression continues to be an important element of the work you will do with your students during shared reading time.

While your students are able to absorb more sophisticated word work at this point, they still greatly benefit from taking the time to get to know new poems slowly. On the first day that a new poem is introduced, you will find that the class as a whole is more able to read along with you more quickly than it was earlier on in the process. Still, it is important not to dive directly into the word work you may be itching to do. Take the time to discuss what children notice about the poem, both at the word level and in terms of meaning. You may find that children bring up words and patterns on their own. You may find that their comments still focus on meaning. Having a thorough understanding of the poem's meaning is a crucial element of the subsequent word work you'll do.

Focus on Comprehension

You may find that you need not devote an entire lesson to comprehension, as you may have done earlier on in the shared reading process. You might feel that you have adequately addressed issues of comprehension during your introductory day. You may, however, choose to enhance comprehension or work with figurative language and so on by spending some more time throughout the process doing activities or projects based around comprehension. Illustrating poems, acting them out, and writing class poems based on the shared reading poem are all ways that you can build on your students' comprehension at this point.

Building Confidence and Community

Just as in the early stages, reading together lifts the spirits, fills the heart, and centers and connects a group of people. This is no less important at this stage! Children who may struggle to read fluently on their own will also take comfort in reading together and will be able to take risks and try things out that they may not feel comfortable doing alone. The support of the group will encourage and lift the individual, and the group is made stronger by the blend of individual voices.

Focus on Developing an Ear for Rhyme

While children will be more able to connect rhyme that they hear with the way words are made at this point, it is still useful to spend time noticing rhyme out loud and playing games where you ask children to supply the next rhyme in a poem. Rhyme engages children, and looking for and generating rhymes brings a playful tone to this work!

Focus on Letter Identification

At this point in the process, most children will have a solid understanding of consonant letter sounds. Vowels clearly take a longer period of time to master, so you may still choose to provide your students with opportunities to identify vowels and vowel sounds in the poems you are studying. More often, at this point, students will be ready to identify vowels as part of a particular simple spelling pattern or group of spelling patterns. You may have some students who are still developing phonemic awareness, and shared reading provides a great way to differentiate instruction. You can call one child up to a poem to identify a word with the spelling pattern *ink*, for example, and you can call the next child up to identify a word that starts with the letter *w*. Both children are participating, and both children are getting what they need.

Focus on Spelling Patterns

Most children in this phase of shared reading will be able to visually identify simple spelling patterns, first within simple CVC words, and then moving on to more complex patterns in CVCC words. Children are ready to learn consonant digraphs, two-letter consonant blends, and simple word endings like *s* and *ing*. You will also be able to continue children's exploration of vowel sounds by introducing the long vowels created by adding a silent *e*, or "magic *e*," at the end of a word. As with all shared reading work, you will be able to differentiate instruction for your students relatively easily by asking them to interact with the text in ways that lift the level of their thinking, no matter where they are starting from.

Focus on Sight Words

Children are now developing a larger bank of sight words that they will be able to identify in their reading and use in their writing. You may choose to use shared reading poems as a way to introduce new sight words to your students—choosing a poem in which the sight word in question appears multiple times works best for this. You might also choose to use the poems as a way for students to review sight words they are getting to know. Children love to notice familiar words in poems, and this will no doubt be among the first comments children make when you ask them what they notice in a new poem—"I see the word is!" someone will announce with pride and glee. You could extend the sight word work provided by a shared reading poem by incorporating those words into familiar sight word games and activities you may already be playing with your class as well.

The Poems

"Waiting"
>   poem containing spelling patterns *all, ell, ill*
>   sight words: *at, he, his, in, on, that, the, to, with*

"Lunch"
>   poem containing digraphs *ch, sh, th*
>   sight words: *a, and, as, I, of, our, she, that, then, we*

"Missing Shoe"
>   poem containing digraph *wh*
>   sight words: *did, do, I, it, my, of, off, took, was, when, where, who, why, with, you*

"Clock"
>   poem containing digraph *ck*
>   sight words: *and, but, is, me, the, when, with*

"Some Teeth," by Jacob Bortner-Hart
>   sight words: *a, and, are, by, some, when, with*

"A Song I Sang," by Amy Ludwig VanDerwater
>   poem containing spelling patterns *ang, ing, ong, ung*
>   sight words: *a, and, for, I, in, it, me, my, of, on, that, this, to, too, will*

"Poor Frog"
>   poem containing spelling patterns *ank, ink, onk, unk*
>   sight words: *but, him, his, I, is, on, saw, that, the*

"The Last Leaf"
>   poem containing work with endings: adding *ed*
>   sight words: *a, and, go, it, of, on, the, to, up, when, which, with*

"Friends"
>   poem containing work with endings: adding *s* and adding *ing*
>   sight words: *am, but, he, I, like, our, see, the, we, what, when, where, while*

"Stuck Spider"
>   poem containing blends *sk, sm, sp, st*
>   sight words: *a, all, and, do, down, he, his, in, into, of, on, the, to, took, was*

"Two Poems," by Elizabeth Heisner
> poems containing blends *fl, pl, sl*
> sight words: *and, are, by, down, in, me, of, the, to*

"Dream"
> poem containing blends *dr, fr, pr, tr*
> sight words: *a, and, as, by, for, her, I, me, my, so, that, they, us, we*

"The Window Pane," by Nicole Callihan
> poem containing long vowel *a: a–e*
> sight words: *a, all, an, and, as, ever, go, going, it, just, like, my, on, the,*
>> *then, will*

"Microscope"
> poem containing long vowel *o: o–e*
> sight words: *a, and, are, at, from, have, I, just, look, me, my, of, them, this, up,*
>> *what, will*

"Five Mice," by Elizabeth Heisner
> poem containing long vowel *i: i–e*
> sight words: *a, an, and, before, but, could, down, fine, he, his, how, in, into, is, most,*
>> *nice, not, now, of, one, or, our, she, so, some, than, that, the, then, they, to, where*

Waiting

Spelling patterns: *all, ell, ill*
Sight words: *at, he, his, in, on, that, the, to, with*

> ### Waiting
> The horse waits in his stall
> at the end of the hall
> in the barn at the top of the hill.
> He rests his chin on the windowsill,
> munches oats until he's had his fill
> and doesn't care that lots of them spill.
> He waits in his stall
> for the boy with the bell
> to lose his ball down the wishing well
> and come instead to pat his head
> in the very last stall
> at the end of the hall
> in the barn at the top of the hill.

Curricular Goals for "Waiting"

Following is a list of possible curricular goals to be accomplished with this poem. You need not spend a lesson on each goal. Devote your lessons to meeting those curricular goals that will best serve your particular class.

- introductory work
- focus on comprehension
- building confidence and community
- focus on developing an ear for rhyme
- focus on letter identification
- focus on spelling patterns
- focus on sight words

Primary Curricular Goals

- focus on spelling patterns: *all*, *ell*, *ill*

Previously Covered

- introductory work
- focus on comprehension
- building confidence and community
- focus on developing an ear for rhyme
- focus on letter identification

Setup

- Gather your students together on the rug or at your class meeting place so that they will all be able to see the words of the poem.

- Have your pointer available and a dry-erase board and dry-erase marker ready (chalk and a chalkboard work fine, too!).

Introduction

- Tell your students that after you read through the poem together, you are going to pay attention to the words with *all*, *ell*, and *ill* in them. (Choose just one if that suits the needs of your class.)

- Show them where on your board you have written *all*, *ell*, and *ill*.

Interacting with the Text

- Read the poem once through with your class, pointing below the words. Ask your students to follow along with their eyes and voices as you read.

- Tell them that you are going to be asking students to come up and read the words with *all*, *ell*, and *ill* in them, but that first you want to practice.

- Demonstrate reading each of the patterns, pointing below where you've written them on the board. Ask students to read along with you.

- Show students that they can read many words if they recognize those patterns: "If you can read *all*, you can read *ball*!" Add a consonant to the beginning of *all* and demonstrate reading it. Change the consonant and ask a child to read the word. Do the same with the other endings (or stick with one, as previously mentioned).

- Tell students that they can use what they know about those endings to read the *all*, *ell*, and *ill* words in the poem. Ask for volunteers to come up, point below one of the words, and read it to the class.

■ Continue until all of those words have been read or until your class is ready to move on to something else.

From the Classroom: Drawing in Children Who Are Not Reading Along

Often certain children have difficulty focusing and reading along with the class during shared reading time. This may not be immediately obvious to you, especially as you are doing several things at once—pointing to the words, reading in a strong, clear voice, and trying to pay attention to all of your students' experiences as you read. One of Sylvia's first graders, Thomas, is such a child. He doesn't draw attention to himself; in fact, he seems to do what he can to avoid it! Sylvia has been working with him to help him feel more comfortable raising his hand and sharing his ideas in the large group. She has recently noticed that during shared reading time, Thomas tends to look slightly away from the poem. He does not often say the words along with the class, even after Sylvia explained to the class why shared reading is an important time to be a talker, not just a listener. Sylvia is unsure what might be getting in the way for Thomas. Perhaps the amount of oral language is overwhelming for him and he shuts down. Perhaps he is busy imagining something else. Perhaps he feels intimidated by the act of reading aloud. Sylvia does know that when she encourages Thomas to read along with the class, he appears to be embarrassed, no matter how gently she reminds him. She decided to have a conversation with him and develop a small visual cue to help him realize when he has drifted away from saying the poem. She has told him that when she notices that he seems to be thinking about other things besides the poem, she will catch his eye and make a small gesture with her hand that looks like a puppet mouth opening and closing. That way, she tells him, she won't need to say his name out loud, and she won't have to stop reading the poem.

"OK, everyone, let's read through 'Waiting' one more time. Thomas, keep your eye out for our secret sign!"

The class begins reading the poem. Thomas' eyes are on the poem at first, and he does read the first couple of lines with the class, but he is soon looking over to the side and has stopped saying words. Sylvia continues pointing, but she reaches out and gives Thomas the secret sign. He smiles and looks quickly back at the poem. He is familiar enough with the poem to join in right then.

As the class reads, Thomas' attention drifts once more, and once more Sylvia gives him the secret sign.

Sylvia suspects that once Thomas gets used to being expected to read along each time, she'll need to use the sign less and less, but she wants to hold him to it throughout the poem now so that he internalizes the activity.

Extending Your Class' Work with "Waiting"

■ This poem was designed with a strong beat. As your students become more familiar with the words, you can ask them to clap in time as you all read the words together. Paying attention to the poem's rhythm not only is fun but also can build momentum and draw children in as they read, encouraging them to take more risks.

▪ The horse in the poem is tired of waiting for the little boy to come. As a comprehension-deepening exercise, have your students think of a time when they had to wait for someone to come or for something to happen. Have them tell this waiting story to a neighbor on the rug.

Lunch

Spelling patterns: digraphs *ch*, *sh*, *th*
Sight words: *a, and, as, I, of, our, she, that, then, we*

> ### Lunch
> I choose cherries.
> She chooses cheese.
> I choose chocolate.
> She chooses three
> sweet plums
> and a bunch of grapes.
> Then we sit to lunch:
> we crunch
> and munch
> as we chew
> and chat.
> Then we wash
> our hands
> and that's the end
> of that!

Curricular Goals for "Lunch"

Following is a list of possible curricular goals to be accomplished with this poem. You need not spend a lesson on each goal. Devote your lessons to meeting those curricular goals that will best serve your particular class.

- introductory work
- focus on comprehension
- building confidence and community
- focus on developing an ear for rhyme
- focus on letter identification
- focus on spelling patterns
- focus on sight words

Primary Curricular Goals

- focus on spelling pattern: *ch*

Previously Covered

- introductory work
- focus on comprehension
- building confidence and community
- focus on developing an ear for rhyme
- focus on letter identification

Setup

- Before this lesson, cover up (with sticky notes, paper and tape, or blank labels) all the places where *ch* occurs in the poem.
- Gather your students together on the rug or at your class meeting place so that they will all be able to see the words of the poem.

Introduction

- Tell your students that when they listen to you reading the poem today, it will sound a little bit strange because something important is missing. Tell them that their job will be to listen hard as you read and to see if they can figure out what two letters have been taken away from some words in the poem.

Interacting with the Text

- Read the poem through, accentuating the missing /ch/ sound in each word. Children are likely to find this quite hilarious, so you may need to refocus them.
- Ask students if they have a guess about what two letters are missing. If students seem confused by this, you may choose to isolate one word—lunch, for example—and ask students what sound is missing from the end of the word. Once they have isolated the missing sound, ask them what two letters make that sound. It is likely that someone will know, because you have probably been drawing the class' attention to these digraphs during other times in the day.
- Once students have agreed that the digraph *ch* is missing, invite individuals to come up to the poem and write it in.
- When the students have finished adding in the *ch*s, read the poem through together.

Extending Your Class' Work with "Lunch"

- This poem lends itself well to dramatizing with props or pictures—a technique that is especially helpful for ELLs. Having pairs of children act the poem out using props in front of the class can be a very motivating way for children to learn the poem.

■ Ask your students to write a list of what they would choose for their favorite lunch. (See Figure 2–1.)

■ Ask your students to illustrate the poem.

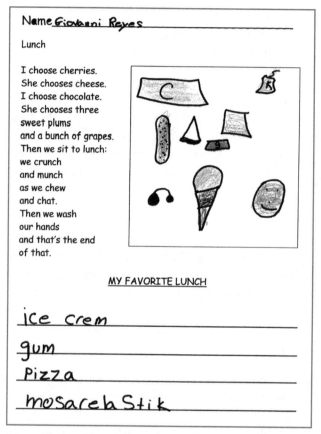

Name Giovanni Reyes

Lunch

I choose cherries.
She chooses cheese.
I choose chocolate.
She chooses three
sweet plums
and a bunch of grapes.
Then we sit to lunch:
we crunch
and munch
as we chew
and chat.
Then we wash
our hands
and that's the end
of that.

MY FAVORITE LUNCH

ice crem

gum

Pizza

mosarelaStik

Figure 2–1   Giovanni's list of his favorite lunch foods

Missing Shoe

Spelling patterns: *i–e, wh*
Review sight words: *did, do, I, it, my, of, off, took, was, with, you*
Newer sight words: *when, where, who, why*

> ### Missing Shoe
> Who took my shoe?
> Was it you?
> Was it you?
> Who took my shoe?
> With it, what did you do?
> Where did you hide it?
> Why did you slide it
> off of my foot
> when I was talking to you?

Curricular Goals for "Missing Shoe"

Following is a list of possible curricular goals to be accomplished with this poem. You need not spend a lesson on each goal. Devote your lessons to meeting those curricular goals that will best serve your particular class.

- introductory work
- focus on comprehension
- building confidence and community
- focus on developing an ear for rhyme
- focus on letter identification
- focus on spelling patterns
- focus on sight words

Noticing wh: A Lesson Using "Missing Shoe"

Primary Curricular Goals

- focus on spelling pattern: *wh*

Previously Covered

- introductory work
- focus on comprehension
- building confidence and community
- focus on developing an ear for rhyme
- focus on letter identification

Setup

- Gather your students together on the rug or at your class meeting place so that they will all be able to see the words of the poem.
- Have your pointer available as well as your choice of materials for the children to use when marking the letters *wh* in the text (transparent colored tape, wax strips, or marker).

Introduction

- Tell your students that because they have gotten to know the poem "Missing Shoe" so well, they will be searching out the /wh/ sound together. If you have been drawing their attention to this digraph at other times in the day (this is always a good idea!), you can remind them of other places they've seen it.

- Tell them that after you read the poem together, you'll be asking individuals to come up and mark just the *wh* in each wh word.

Interacting with the Text

- Ask your students to read the poem with you; there is no need to read it to them alone first, as they will have had other opportunities to read it before you attempt this lesson.

- Ask your students to turn and whisper in their neighbor's ear if they see a word that has *wh* in it.

- Ask a student to share the word she noticed.

- Invite individuals to come to the front of the room and mark the *wh* in one word.

From the Classroom: Engaging All Students Through Counting wh Words

Finding new ways to engage all children in an activity on the rug can be a challenge. Sometimes very quick and simple twists in the usual routine can do the trick. In the example that follows, Tim decides to have his students count all of the *wh* words that individuals have covered with transparent tape. This perks up especially some of the more mathematically minded of his first graders. Tim has asked his students to read the poem together one more time and to put their thumbs up when their eyes touch a word with *wh* in it.

"I saw lots of thumbs going up and down as we read together. Looks like you found lots of *wh* words in there! I wonder how many there are. Do you think we can count them?"

"Yes!" the students agree.

"Let's try this: I'll read the poem by myself, and you guys keep track on your fingers of each word I read that has *wh* in it. Count on your fingers. OK?"

Tim reads the poem slowly, watching the kids count *wh* words on their fingers as they go. When he's done reading, he asks the kids to turn and tell their neighbors on the rug how many they counted, and then he asks the whole class to tell him how many the students found. They generally agree that there are six and count out loud together as Tim points out the words with the wand.

Extending Your Class' Work with "Missing Shoe"

- Have two students act out the poem as the rest of the class reads it out loud. They'll love getting to steal each other's shoes!

- During transitions on the rug, ask individuals or small teams of kids to read the poem aloud to the rest of the class.

- Ask your students to tell (or write) the story behind the silly situation: Why is someone stealing the speaker's shoe? Will he give it back? What does the thief plan to do with it?

- The poem might be used again as a source for reviewing the long *i* sound, in the spelling pattern *i–e*. Since it occurs only twice in the poem, it's not the best way to introduce the pattern, but it works nicely as a tool for review. You might read through the poem together twice as a class, and then after reminding students of the long *i* or *i–e* pattern, have individual students highlight relevant words as they appear in the poem. You might then generate a list of *i–e* words together.

A List of wh Words Generated by Class 1-115

After the class has been spying out *wh* words all week, in the context of "Missing Shoe" and in the books the students read during reading workshop, Tim has asked them to generate a list together of all of the words they can think of that start with *wh*.

Because the /wh/ sound is very similar to the /w/ sound, several students offer words that begin with *w* in addition to *wh* words. This provides a great opportunity for the class to generate two lists and to compare them. When a student offers a *w* word, Tim explains how tricky it is to distinguish between the two sounds and starts another list of *w* words so that the kids can see the difference. Children who have a more sophisticated understanding will be able to contribute *wh* words, and students who need practice with *w* words will still be able to participate and to contribute words to a list.

The class now has a resource list that can hang in the room and help the kids during reading and writing time. (See Figure 2–2.)

1-115's List of *w* Words and *wh* Words	
w Words	*wh* Words
wish	where
walk	who
worry	when
Washington	why
William	whistle
we	whale
wink	whirl
weather	whip
wiggle	

Figure 2–2 *Class 1-115's chart of* w *and* wh *words*

Clock

Spelling pattern: *ck*
Sight words: *and, but, is, me, the, when, with*

> **Clock**
> The clock's
> tick-tock
> tells me when is now.
> But with each
> tock's tick
> and each
> tick's tock,
> now changes
> into then!

Curricular Goals for "Clock"

Following is a list of possible curricular goals to be accomplished with this poem. You need not spend a lesson on each goal. Devote your lessons to meeting those curricular goals that will best serve your particular class.

- introductory work
- focus on comprehension
- building confidence and community
- focus on developing an ear for rhyme
- focus on letter identification
- focus on spelling pattern
- focus on sight words

Figuring Out ck: A Lesson Using "Clock"

Primary Curricular Goals

- focus on spelling pattern: *ck*

Previously Covered

- ▪ introductory work
- ▪ focus on comprehension
- ▪ building confidence and community
- ▪ focus on developing an ear for rhyme
- ▪ focus on letter identification

Setup

- ▪ In a previous lesson, you will have asked students to notice and highlight or underline those words in "Clock" that contain the digraph *ck*.
- ▪ Gather your students together on the rug or at your class meeting place so that they will all be able to see the words of the poem.

Introduction

- ▪ Tell your students that because they have already spent time getting to know the poem "Clock," and have marked the words in the poem that contain the digraph *ck*, you will now be investigating when and where the digraph *ck* is usually found. (You will want them to discover that *ck* is found at the end of the word, never at the beginning, and that it has a vowel in front of it.)

Interacting with the Text

- ▪ Read the poem once through with your students, pointing below the words. Ask your students to follow along with their eyes and voices as you read.

- ▪ Ask several students to read from their seats the words that contain the digraph *ck*.

- ▪ Tell your students that because *ck* sounds just like *k*, they will need to do a little detective work to start figuring out when and where *ck* is used. Ask them if they notice any similarities in the words they've highlighted.

- ▪ Some students may easily notice that the *ck* is always found at the end of the word. Some may even notice that there is a vowel in front of it. If your students are having a difficult time noticing these things, you may want to write the words in a list on a separate piece of paper so that the pattern is easier to recognize. If your students are still not noticing, ask them, "Where in the words do you see the *ck*?" or "What kind of a letter do you always see before the *ck*?"—this is not likely to be necessary, though.

- ▪ You may want to challenge your students to think of words that begin with *ck* to prove their theory. Any words they suggest could be written up in a separate place—*k* words together, *c* words together, and so on.

Sarah's students have been having an engaging discussion about the placement of the digraph *ck* in words. They have agreed on a theory that *ck* is always at the end of a word, and they have noticed that there is always a vowel in front of it. Sarah would like to go a bit deeper and to solidify the children's theory.

"So you're all agreed that *ck* is at the end of the word in the *ck* words from 'Clock,' but I am wondering about other words. Here's a challenge: Can anyone think of any words they know that begin with *ck*? We'll start a list." Sarah gets a big piece of chart paper ready.

"How about *kick*?" asks Charles when Sarah calls on him.

"That starts with *k*," Georgia interrupts.

"Hand, please, Georgia—try again." She does, and Sarah calls on her, and she says her idea again.

"Actually, you're right, Georgia. *Kick* does start with *k*, but it does end with *ck*, Charles. Let's write *kick* right here. OK, anyone else think of a word that starts with *ck*?" After calling on a few kids and adding *kit* and *kid* to the list of words under *kick*, and *crack*, *candle*, and *cart* to another column of words starting with *c*, Sarah asks the kids what they think.

"I think we were right," Wayne says. "I think you can't start words with *ck*."

"Thumbs up if you agree with Wayne," Sarah says. All of the thumbs go up. "Anyone want to say anything else before we move on?" she continues.

"I think *kick* and *crack* are like the other words in the clock poem," says Hannah.

"What do you mean, Hannah?"

"Well, the *ck* is at the end, and there's a vowel right in front, like the other words we found in the poem."

"Goodness, look at that!" Sarah says with amazement.

"But what about *chicken*?" Georgia interrupts.

"Hand, Georgia," Sarah reminds her.

After raising her hand and being called on, Georgia says, "I think *chicken* has a *ck*, but it's not at the end."

Sarah writes the word *chicken* up in a third column on the chart paper.

"Look at that, everyone. *Chicken* does in fact have a *ck* in it, but it isn't at the end of the word! Now what are we supposed to think?" Several gasps come from the first graders on the rug, quickly followed by lots of talking. Because the class is about to be late for art, Sarah tells the children that they can continue their investigation later in the day.

Extending Your Class' Work with "Clock"

■ Connect this poem with a simple lesson on telling time, if appropriate for your class.

■ Post the poem next to your classroom clock so that children can see it!

Some Teeth

Sight words: *a, and, are, by, some, when, with*

> ### Some Teeth
> Some teeth are shiny.
> Some teeth are white.
> Some teeth are clean,
> Glowing and bright.
>
> Some teeth are dirty.
> Some teeth are black.
> Some teeth are filthy
> Covered with plaque.
>
> Some teeth are light.
> Some teeth are dark.
> Some teeth are deadly
> When owned by a shark!
> —*Jacob Bortner-Hart*
> *(when he was in third grade)*

Curricular Goals for "Some Teeth"

Following is a list of possible curricular goals to be accomplished with this poem. You need not spend a lesson on each goal. Devote your lessons to meeting those curricular goals that will best serve your particular class.

- introductory work
- focus on comprehension
- building confidence and community
- focus on developing an ear for rhyme
- focus on letter identification
- focus on spelling patterns
- focus on sight words

Primary Curricular Goals

- focus on sight word: *some*

Previously Covered

- introductory work
- focus on comprehension
- building confidence and community
- focus on developing an ear for rhyme
- focus on letter identification

Setup

- Before the lesson, cover up many (maybe every other) *some*s in Jacob's poem. Write the word *some* on cards that children will be able to tape to the chart in the appropriate place later on. Also write other sight words on similar cards so that children need to look carefully in order to choose the appropriate word.

- Gather your students together on the rug or at your class meeting place so that they will all be able to see the words of the poem.

- You'll need some tape to stick the words on the chart.

Introduction

- Tell your students that they are going to be using Jacob's poem, "Some Teeth," to practice finding and reading the new sight word *some*. Tell them you've covered up some of the words in the poem, and that after reading it through together, children will have an opportunity to find and fill in the missing words.

Interacting with the Text

- Read the poem through together. You will want to have read this poem through together before, so that children know the poem's pattern and are able to read along even though so many *some*s are missing.

- Ask individuals to come up and look through your collection of sight word cards to find the word *some* and stick it onto the chart in an appropriate place.

- Once all of the missing words have been filled in, read the poem through together again.

■ Have students draw all of the kinds of teeth they know. Encourage them to think like Jacob did: What do sharks' teeth look like? How about alligators'? How about beavers'?

■ Have your children write their own "some" poems. Brainstorm objects of which there exist many different kinds—dogs, pens, cars, and so on. Have your students choose an idea and use the word *some* to describe the different representations of what they've chosen. (See Figure 2–3.) If this seems too challenging for your class, just write a class poem using *some* instead.

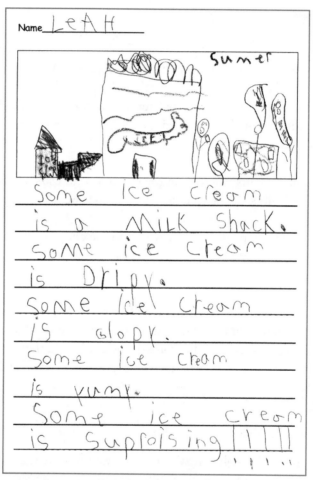

Figure 2–3 *Leah's poem "Some Ice Cream"*

A Song I Sang

Spelling patterns: *ang, ing, ong, ung*
Sight words: *a, and, for, I, in, it, me, my, of, on, that, this, to, too, will*

A Song I Sang
A song I sang
another day
lives in me still
won't fly away.

It built a nest
that song I sung.
It's in my mind.
It's on my tongue.

I've sung it now
for far too long.
I need to learn
a brand new song.

I need to sing
another thing
and hope this song
inside of me
will wave a wing
will soar and sing
Goodbye.
—Amy Ludwig VanDerwater

Curricular Goals for "A Song I Sang"

Following is a list of possible curricular goals to be accomplished with this poem. You need not spend a lesson on each goal. Devote your lessons to meeting those curricular goals that will best serve your particular class.

- introductory work
- focus on comprehension
- building confidence and community
- focus on developing an ear for rhyme
- focus on letter identification
- focus on spelling patterns
- focus on sight words

Let's Sort! A Lesson Using "A Song I Sang"

Primary Curricular Goals

- focus on spelling patterns: *ang, ing, ong, ung*

Previously Covered

- introductory work
- focus on comprehension
- building confidence and community
- focus on developing an ear for rhyme
- focus on letter identification
- focus on spelling patterns: *ang, ing, ong, ung*

Setup

- Prior to this lesson, you will want to have already focused together on the spelling patterns *ang, ing, ong,* and *ung* in the poem—perhaps children have even covered them with transparent colored tape color-coded according to spelling pattern.

- Today, you will want to set up a sorting board that your students will be using to sort the *ang, ing, ong,* and *ung* words appearing in the poem, as well as write those words on cards that children will use to sort. You will want to write up some other simple examples of each of the spelling patterns as well—how many will depend on your class' understanding of the spelling patterns. See Figure 2–4 for a sample sorting board.

- Gather your students together on the rug or at your class meeting place so that they will all be able to see the words of the poem.

Introduction

- Tell your students that after reading through Amy's poem together, you'll be sorting some of the words on the chart you've created, to help kids keep

Word Sort: *ang, ing, ong, ung*			
ang	*ing*	*ong*	*ung*

Figure 2–4 *Sample sorting board*

track of which is which and also to post in the room for them to use when they are writing.

Interacting with the Text

- ■ Read the poem once through together. You may also want to call on children to give examples of words containing each of the four spelling patterns in the poem.

- ■ Show the children the word cards you have made. Model picking a card, looking at the chart, and taping the card in the appropriate column. You may want to ask children to notice how you match up each of the last three letters in the word to make sure you are placing the word correctly.

- ■ Ask individuals to come up and choose a card and then stick the card in the appropriate column on the chart.

- ■ This activity may be repeated multiple times. You may also choose to create a similar sort for students to work on individually.

- ■ A sort chart in process may look something like the one in Figure 2–5.

From the Classroom: Making Individual Sorts with *ang, ing, ong, and* ung

Alice knows that her students could use some more support with learning the spelling patterns presented in the poem "A Song I Sang," and that the experience of participating in a group sorting project was helpful, but not interactive enough for all of her students to begin to internalize the work. She has decided to create individual sorting kits to be used as a center activity during her weekly word study choice time. She makes five individual boards—smaller versions of the chart she'd

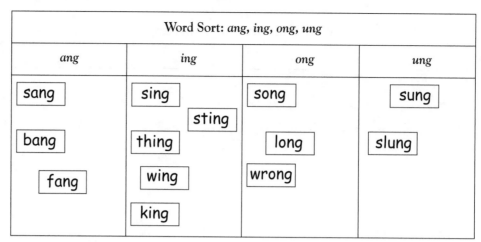

Figure 2–5 *A sorting chart in progress*

used with the whole class earlier—and little versions of the sorting cards as well, which she keeps in little mint boxes she's collected. (You can also find commercially designed sorts of this nature.) When Alice makes the sorting cards, she includes appropriate words from Alice's poem, and she includes a few more words as well. Alice introduces the activity to a group she thinks would benefit from this kind of hands-on work during word study choice time. Amy also has a small printed copy of the poem available for the kids to use as a reference if they like.

"OK, everyone, remember a couple of days ago when we were sorting the words in Amy's poem during shared reading? Well, I made a tiny version for each of you to use so that you can sort all of the words on your own. It's OK with me if you work together on this, too—it's up to you this time. Here's how it works. Everyone make sure your board is in front of you." The kids all take a board and put it on the table in front of them.

"Now, open your word containers." The kids do so with the glee young children have for using their own miniature supplies. Mohammed, in fact, begins to dump out the contents of his container and spread the words around.

"Hold up, Mohammed. We're going to take words out one at a time here, so you can keep track of which ones you've sorted and which you haven't. Put them back in." Mohammed does.

"So next, everyone take out a card. Tyeesha, what word do you have?"

Tyeesha looks at her word—*sing*—and then up at Alice with a questioning look. "Is that *sing*?" she asks.

"Yep!" Alice says. She's about to respond further when the rest of the kids start talking and reading their words all at once.

"Hold up, first graders," Alice says. "We're not starting yet; let's watch what Tyeesha decides to do first, and then you'll all get to start. Go ahead, Tyeesha. Where do you think that word should go?"

"Here?" Tyeesha says, placing the word in the *ing* column.

"What do you think, guys? Is that where you would put it?"

"Yes!" says Martin.

"Why would you put it there, Martin?"

"Because it has the *i* and then the *n* and then the *g*, like up there," he says, pointing to the column's heading.

"Makes sense to me! Good thinking, Tyeesha. OK, everyone, you can keep going on your own. Have fun!"

Extending Your Class' Work with "A Song I Sang"

■ Make individual sorting games for children to use during center time or other times during the day—maybe you do a word study choice time—using *ang*, *ing*, *ong*, and *ung* words.

■ Have a class conversation about the songs that get stuck in your students' heads. You may even choose to have students bring in examples of these songs to play for the class!

Poor Frog

Spelling patterns: *ank, ink, onk, unk*
Sight words: *but, him, his, I, is, on, saw, that, the*

> ### *Poor Frog*
> The frog stares.
> His face is blank.
> But wait!
> I think
> I saw him blink!
> Kerplunk!
> I heard him jump!
> Bonk!
> He bumped his head
> on the log
> that is his bed.
> Poor frog!

Curricular Goals for "Poor Frog"

Following is a list of possible curricular goals to be accomplished with this poem. You need not spend a lesson on each goal. Devote your lessons to meeting those curricular goals that will best serve your particular class.

- introductory work
- focus on comprehension
- building confidence and community
- focus on developing an ear for rhyme
- focus on letter identification
- focus on spelling patterns
- focus on sight words

Generating ank, ink, onk, *and* unk *Words: A Lesson Using "Poor Frog"*

Primary Curricular Goals

- focus on spelling patterns: *ank*, *ink*, *onk*, *unk*

Previously Covered

- introductory work
- focus on comprehension
- building confidence and community
- focus on developing an ear for rhyme
- focus on letter identification

Setup

- Before the lesson, prepare a chart with four columns, each labeled with one of the spelling patterns you are studying. (See Figure 2–6.)
- Gather your students together on the rug or at your class meeting place so that they will all be able to see the words of the poem.

Introduction

- Tell your students that after they read the poem through together, they will be adding words to the chart you've started.

Interacting with the Text

- Read through the poem together once.

- You may choose to read through the poem again and ask children to particularly notice words that end in *ank*, *ink*, *onk*, and *unk*.

- Ask individual students to first identify a word that ends in one of the focus spelling patterns and then to come up and write it in the appropriate column of your chart.

***ank* Words**	***ink* Words**	***onk* Words**	***unk* Words**

Figure 2–6 *Spelling pattern chart*

ank Words	*ink* Words	*onk* Words	*unk* Words
tank	blink	honk	junk
thank	think	bonk	clunk
blank	wink		kerplunk
blanket	stinky		
	link		

Figure 2–7 *Sample spelling pattern chart*

- When all of the relevant words from the poem have been added to the chart, ask children to generate other words they know that end in one of those ways and to come up to the chart and add them on.

- Read through the chart as a class (see example in Figure 2–7).

- If you prefer, focus on one spelling pattern at a time and stretch this activity out over several days.

From the Classroom: Tips for Encouraging Awareness of Spelling Patterns Throughout the Day

Class 1-226 has been reading the poem "Poor Frog" for four days. As a transition activity between reading and writing time, Sarah has her students act out the poem on the rug as they read the poem together; she knows that they will be able to move and read simultaneously because they know the poem well. First, she asks the students to spread out so that they have at least an arm's length between them. When they are settled, she asks them to get into "frog position." Twenty-six first graders pop up on their feet and crouch with their knees stuck out to the side. Sarah can't help but grin at them.

"OK, guys, remember, as we read, your job is to fit what your body is doing with the words of the poem. And when we get to the jumping part, make sure that you don't jump into anyone else's space. Let's go!"

They begin to read, "The frog stares. / His face is blank." Twenty-six blank-faced frogs stare straight ahead (except for Tomas, who is having a hard time not giggling).

The class and Sarah continue, "But wait! / I think / I saw him blink!" Twenty-six blinking frogs look up at her. "Kerplunk! / I heard him jump!" The frogs pop up into the air. There is, as Sarah expected, a flurry of laughter and wobbling as the kids resettle themselves in frog position. She waits to begin the next line until they are all looking up at her again.

Figure 2–8 *Children acting out the poem "Poor Frog"*

"Bonk! / He bumped his head / on the log / that is his bed." Twenty-six frogs pantomime bumping their heads. Wilbur crosses his eyes expertly. Sylvie, watching him, laughs her big belly laugh.

Sarah gathers the kids' attention by pointing at the last line on the chart paper and saying, "OK, all together . . . *Poor frog!*"

Because the poem is a short one and its dramatization involves no setup beyond asking the kids to get into frog position, Sarah agrees that they have time for "just once more" when her first graders ask.

Extending Your Class' Work with "Poor Frog"

■ Instead of (or in addition to) focusing on the *ank*, *ink*, *onk*, and *unk* spelling patterns, draw your students' attention to the blends *bl* and *pl*.

■ Have your students illustrate the poem in storyboard form. The poem has a very distinct sequence, and children will be able to practice thinking about the beginning, middle, and end of a story as they draw.

■ Using the *ank*, *ink*, *onk*, and *unk* spelling patterns and the lists of relevant words your class has generated, work together to create a short story using as many of those words as possible. You may want to write most of the story on chart paper yourself as the students tell it, but you also may choose to turn the activity into an opportunity for interactive writing, encouraging individuals to come up and share the pen when you come to words that contain the relevant spelling patterns.

The Last Leaf

Endings: adding *ed*
Sight words: *a, and, go, it, of, on, the, to, up, when, which, with*

> ### The Last Leaf
> When the wind wound up,
> the tree let go of its last red leaf,
> which curled
> and swirled
> and jiggled
> and whirled,
> which jumped
> and bumped
> and wiggled
> and slumped
> gently
> side to side
> until it landed with a whisper
> on the step.

Curricular Goals for "The Last Leaf"

Following is a list of possible curricular goals to be accomplished with this poem. You need not spend a lesson on each goal. Devote your lessons to meeting those curricular goals that will best serve your particular class.

- introductory work
- focus on comprehension
- building confidence and community
- focus on developing an ear for rhyme
- focus on letter identification
- focus on spelling patterns
- focus on suffix: adding *ed*
- focus on sight words

Primary Curricular Goals

- focus on suffix: adding *ed*

Previously Covered

- introductory work
- focus on comprehension
- focus on developing an ear for rhyme
- focus on letter identification
- focus on spelling patterns

Setup

- You will want to have done a lesson previously in which you asked students to identify and mark the *ed* ending in words (e.g., with transparent tape), so the base words will be easier to see today.

- Gather your students together on the rug or at your class meeting place so that they will all be able to see the words of the poem.

- Have available a piece of chart paper that you will be able to use for creating a chart that will allow a place for you to write the base word, *ed*, and the base word plus *ed*. You may want to label the columns as shown in Figure 2–9. I prefer leaving the labels off until the class has started building the chart together so that the students can start to see the pattern first. Adding the labels after this can make the chart more meaningful.

Introduction

- Tell your students that after you read the poem once through together, you will again be paying particular attention to the words in the poem that end in the letters *ed*.

Interacting with the Text

- Read the poem once through with your students. They will have had enough experiences with the poem to be able to read along with you confidently.

Base Word	*ed*	Base Word + *ed*

Figure 2–9   *Base words chart*

- Tell your students that next you'll be reading just all of the words that end in *ed* and that they may join you if they like (children might not all be able to recognize the words without reading them in the context of the whole poem).

- After reading just the *ed* words, remind them that *ed* is added to a word to change it from a word that means something happening now to something that already happened.

- Ask them to look at and think about the *ed* words in the poem, and to see if they can figure out what each word was before *ed* was added. If many children are unable to read the words, read them out loud and make this exercise more of a listening activity. Practice with a few words so that children are starting to hear, for example, that "curled" with out the *ed* is "curl" and that "jumped" without the *ed* is "jump."

- Once children are getting the hang of separating the base word from the ed in your conversation, start filling in your chart. You might want to have children come and write the words themselves, or you may fill in the chart as they suggest words. (Figure 2–10 is a sample filled-in chart.)

- When a child suggests either *wiggled* or *jiggled*, as someone most likely will, have a conversation about how this type of word works differently. This poem is meant to be a simple introduction to adding *ed*, so it is assumed in this lesson that children will not have had much exposure to the different things that happen when *ed* is added. You may choose to go into the rule that applies to words that end in *e* already (drop the *e* and add *ed*), or you may choose to save that for another time, depending on the needs of your class.

- Ask your students to look out for words like these in their independent reading; as times passes, this is likely to lead you eventually into a discussion of adding *ed* to CVC words (you have to double the last letter before adding *ed*).

Base Word	*ed*	Base Word + *ed*
curl	ed	curled
swirl	ed	swirled
whirl	ed	whirled
bump	ed	bumped
jump	ed	jumped
wiggle	(drop the *e*, add *ed*)	wiggled

Figure 2–10 *Completed base words chart*

- Ask your students to notice all of the words they find with *ed* endings in the books they read during readers workshop. You can use these collected words to frame a discussion about the different things that can happen when *ed* is added to words (double the last letter, drop the *e* and add *ed*, etc.), if this is appropriate for your class.

- Have the class brainstorm more action words to describe how a leaf might move as it falls from a tree. Together, add *ed* to those words (if the children have not automatically done so). Write your own "falling leaf" poem using those words!

Friends

Spelling patterns: adding *s*, adding *ing*
Sight words: *am, but, he, I, like, our, see, the, we, what, when, where, while*

> ### Friends
>
> He cooks while I am cooking.
> He thinks while I am thinking.
> He looks where I am looking,
> but we see different things.
>
> He runs while I am running.
> He suns while I am sunning.
> He reads while I am reading,
> but we read different things.
>
> He chooses while I am choosing,
> sometimes loses when I'm losing,
> often wins when I am winning,
> sometimes likes what I am liking,
> but our difference is the thing
> we like the best!

Curricular Goals for "Friends"

Following is a list of possible curricular goals to be accomplished with this poem. You need not spend a lesson on each goal. Devote your lessons to meeting those curricular goals that will best serve your particular class.

- introductory work
- focus on comprehension
- building confidence and community
- focus on developing an ear for rhyme
- focus on letter identification
- focus on spelling patterns

- focus on suffixes: adding *s*, adding *ing*
- focus on sight words

Identifying Sight Words Using the Mystery Sight Word Bag: A Lesson Using "Friends"

Primary Curricular Goals

- focus on sight words

Previously Covered

- introductory work
- focus on comprehension
- building confidence and community

Setup

- Before the lesson, write several of the sight words appearing in the poem on cards and place them inside a brown paper bag—the mystery sight word bag. *When, where, while,* and *what* are usually useful within the time frame you may be using this poem, but choose words that will be beneficial to your particular class. You might want to put in more than one card with a particular word that appears frequently in the poem—*while,* for example.

- Gather your students together on the rug or at your class meeting place so that they will all be able to see the words of the poem.

Introduction

- Tell your students that after you read the poem through once or twice together, you will be using the mystery sight word bag to match the words in the bag with sight words in the poem.

Interacting with the Text

- Read the poem through together once or twice as a class.

- Take out your mystery word bag and shake it up dramatically. Tell your students that individuals will be able to come up and pull a word out of the bag, read it, and match it up with the same word in the poem. You may want to have students tape the word card over the word in the poem or just to line it up momentarily after they read and then set it elsewhere.

- Call on individuals to come up and choose a word. After an individual has read a word and matched it up, have the whole class spell the word together.

- Do this for as long as makes sense for your class—often three or four words is plenty. This lesson can be repeated more than once.

After reading this poem a few times with his class, Tim decides to break from the word work and focus on a community-building opportunity. Lately there have been some rumblings of teasing coming up in the class, mostly happening at outside playtime and at lunchtime, and Tim wants to make sure to not only address the teasing directly but also insert some new ideas into the class conversation. The poem they're studying during shared reading time presents a simple entryway into a conversation about difference. Tim decides, after the class reads the poem twice through, to open up a discussion.

"So, first graders. Do you think the kids in this poem are pretty good friends?"

"Yes," Julia says when called on.

"How can you tell, Julia?"

"They do the same things at the same time. They just like each other!"

"They do seem to be doing some of the same things at the same time, but are they doing those things exactly the same way? Cal?"

"No, they like to read different books, and they see different things, too, when they are looking around."

"I noticed that, too. I'm wondering if any of you have a friend that is very different from you. Lots of times friends like to do some of the same things, but do you have to be exactly alike to be friends, everyone?"

"No!" says the class.

"So, let's hear about some of your friends who are different from you. Sam, tell us about your friend."

"My friend Penny is from pre-K and she's a girl. So we're different. But she likes to draw, so we're kind of alike."

"Yep, girls and boys are different from each other, but they definitely can be friends, just like in our class! How about you, Kayla? Tell us about your friend who is different from you."

"My friend Alma from Mr. Ed's class, she is always climbing around on things when we have recess together. She is always climbing up on top of the monkey bars. But I don't like to do that. So when she's done doing that, we play after."

"Aha—so you and Alma don't always like to do the same things at the same time, but you're still friends, right?"

The conversation continues, with various children sharing their experiences of being friends with people who are different.

Extending Your Class' Work with "Friends"

■ Have your students draw pictures of their friends who are different from themselves.

■ Have your students write "She (he) likes to/I like to" comparisons. You can model this for them. Have a volunteer think about a friend who likes some different things, and write a line stating, "She likes to . . . ," followed by a line stating what the student likes to do. For example:

- He likes to ride scooters.
- I like to ride bikes. (See Figure 2–11.)

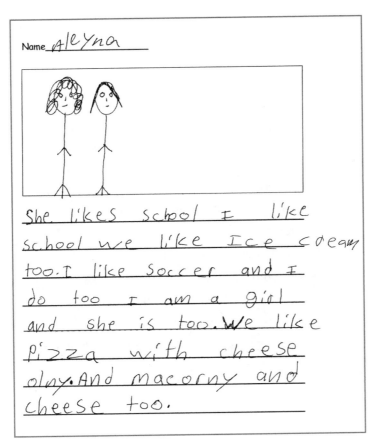

Name Aleyna

She likes school I like
school we like Ice cream
too. I like soccer and I
do too I am a girl
and she is too. We like
pizza with cheese
olny. And macorny and
cheese too.

Figure 2–11 *Aleyna's "She likes/I like" poem*

Stuck Spider

Spelling patterns: blends *sk, sm, sp, st*
Sight words: *a, all, and, do, down, he, his, in, into, of, on, the, to, took, was*

> ### Stuck Spider
> The spider was stuck on the sticky stem.
> He couldn't take a step.
> He couldn't speak or spin his web.
> All he could do was stare.
> Stuck on his stem, he stared into the air.
> He started to make a plan.
> He took eight slippery sticks and quickly fixed
> one to each of his feet.
> Then he sped down the stem in style:
> the first spider using skis!

Curricular Goals for "Stuck Spider"

Following is a list of possible curricular goals to be accomplished with this poem. You need not spend a lesson on each goal. Devote your lessons to meeting those curricular goals that will best serve your particular class.

- introductory work
- focus on comprehension
- building confidence and community
- focus on developing an ear for rhyme
- focus on letter identification
- focus on spelling patterns
- focus on sight words

Highlighting the Blends sk, sm, sp, st: A Lesson Using "Stuck Spider"

Primary Curricular Goals

- focus on spelling patterns: *sk, sm, sp, st*

Previously Covered

- introductory work
- focus on comprehension
- building confidence and community
- focus on developing an ear for rhyme
- focus on letter identification
- focus on spelling patterns: blends *sl, sm, sp, st*
- focus on sight words

Setup

- In a previous lesson, you will want to have highlighted the blends *sk, sm, sp, st* in the poem on chart paper together (e.g., using colored transparent tape).

- Gather your students together on the rug or at your class meeting place so that they will all be able to see the words of the poem.

- Have prepared copies of the poem "Stuck Spider" that students will be able to work with on their own after you read together.

- Have four different colors of crayons available for students to use at their tables; it's best if the crayons match the color of the tape (or marker) that you've used previously to identify the blends in the poem on the chart paper.

Introduction

- Tell your students that after you read the poem through once or twice together, they will each be able to look at a copy of the poem at their table and work together to highlight the blends that they have been noticing in the poem already.

Interacting with the Text

- Read the poem through once or twice together so that it is fresh in your students' minds.

- Tell them that they will be able to work with their tablemates (or individually or in partnerships if you prefer) to do the same work on copies of the poem as you've done together on the chart paper: they will be coloring over (highlighting) the blends *sk, sm, sp,* and *st* as they find them in the poem.

- Send your students to their tables to do this after you have modeled what this will look like on a printout of the poem yourself. It is fine if students need to look at the poem on chart paper to remind them which blend is what color, or you could make a small color chart for the center of each table (see Figure 2–12).

Figure 2–12 *Color-coding chart*

■ When students have finished highlighting the blends, you might ask them to read the poem through once to a partner.

Extending Your Class' Work with "Stuck Spider"

■ Have students draw a picture of a spider on skis.

■ Tie this poem into a nonfiction study in which you read books about spiders and gather information about them: How many legs do they have? How many skis would they need?

Two Poems

Spelling patterns: blends *fl, pl, sl*
Sight words: *and, are, by, down, in, me, of, the, to*

> **Two Poems**
> I.
> flat stones in the stream
> are cleaned by the clear water
> flowing slowly down
>
> II.
> the fledgling clings to the edge
> of the nest and pleads to the wind:
> "Please let me fly!"
> —*Elizabeth Heisner*

Curricular Goals for "Two Poems"

Following is a list of possible curricular goals to be accomplished with this poem. You need not spend a lesson on each goal. Devote your lessons to meeting those curricular goals that will best serve your particular class.

- introductory work
- focus on comprehension
- building confidence and community
- focus on developing an ear for rhyme
- focus on letter identification
- focus on spelling patterns
- focus on sight words

Illustrating the Poems: A Lesson Using "Two Poems"

Primary Curricular Goals

- focus on comprehension

Previously Covered

- introductory work

Setup

- Gather your students together on the rug or at your class meeting place so that they will all be able to see the words of the poem.

- Have prepared papers on which students will illustrate the poems. You may choose to have them do this on plain paper, or you may use a sheet like the one in Figure 2–13.

Introduction

- Tell your students that after you read the poem together, they will be able to add pictures to go along with it.

Interacting with the Text

- Read the poems through once or twice together as a class.

- Read the poems through one more time, asking your students to close their eyes and visualize as you read.

- Tell your students that they will be drawing what they saw when they closed their eyes—illustrating the poem.

- If you are using a special paper, similar to the one in Figure 2–13, show it to your students before they leave the rug.

- Send them to their work seats to illustrate the poem, using whatever illustration tools you prefer. (See Figure 2–14.)

From the Classroom: Noticing fl, pl, and sl Blends Throughout the Day

Providing children with many different contexts in which to experience a new idea, skill, or tool is a wonderful way to help them build confidence and to internalize the new thing you've taught them. Kat has recently introduced the blends *fl*, *pl*, and *sl* to her first graders, and she wants to help them begin to recognize these blends in other contexts besides the poems she used to introduce them. She has invited her students to take sticky notes off to readers workshop so that they can jot down words they notice that use those blends. The children will share what they discovered with the class at the end of readers workshop. She has also invited them to pay attention to their own writing; Colin is very excited to see how often he used the *pl* blend in the word play as he wrote. The kids are now getting lined up to go to the lunchroom, and Kat presents them with a challenge.

Illustrating "Two Poems"

Name_____

Two Poems
by Elizabeth Heisner

I.
flat stones in the stream
are cleaned by the clear water
flowing slowly down

II.
the fledgling clings to the edge
of the nest and pleads to the wind:
"Please let me fly!"

Figure 2–13 *An illustration sheet for "Two Poems"*

Figure 2–14 *Naylan's illustrations of "Two Poems"*

"OK, everyone, stand tall with your partners. Eyes forward please, Betsy. So as we walk to the lunchroom today, I have a challenge for you. We're going to go the long way so that we pass through the lobby where all of the notices are posted, and then down the hall where the second-grade bulletin boards are. I am wondering if we'll see any of those *fl, pl, sl* blends we've been hunting for. We are going to have to walk especially quietly—we can't talk in the hallway, so we're going to have to carry the words we notice in our minds until we get to the lunchroom. Ready? Let's go—keep your eyes open!"

The class makes its slow way to the lunchroom, stopping momentarily before the notice board in the hallway. When they get to the lunchroom, Kat asks volunteers to tell the class what words they saw and where they saw them. Kevin saw, for example, the word *flowers* in the parent-teacher association's notice about the upcoming flower sale fund-raiser. Danny saw *slow* in one of the second graders' stories on the bulletin board. Zadie saw *sleep* in another story.

- Using Elizabeth's poems and perhaps some examples of haiku, have your students write very short poems about elements of nature, focusing primarily on the image.

- Create a word sort for words using the blends *fl, pl,* and *sl*—include both words occurring in the poem and words you've brainstormed as a class that begin with each of those blends.

Dream

Spelling patterns: blends *dr, fr, pr, tr*
Sight words: *a, and, as, by, for, her, I, me, my, that, they, so, us, we*

> ### Dream
> Last night I practiced
> drawing dragons,
> so maybe that is why I dreamed
> that a brave and trusty dragon
> chose me for her flying team.
> We zoomed across the prairie,
> over fruit trees, frogs, and trucks.
> My friends looked up as we flew by.
> They just stood and stared at us!

Curricular Goals for "Dream"

Following is a list of possible curricular goals to be accomplished with this poem. You need not spend a lesson on each goal. Devote your lessons to meeting those curricular goals that will best serve your particular class.

- introductory work
- focus on comprehension
- building confidence and community
- focus on directionality
- focus on words as discrete collections of letters
- focus on developing an ear for rhyme
- focus on letter identification
- focus on spelling patterns
- focus on sight words

Make Your Own Class "Dream" Poem: A Lesson Using "Dream"

Primary Curricular Goals

- focus on spelling pattern: *dr*

- introductory work
- focus on comprehension
- building confidence and community
- focus on directionality
- focus on words as discrete collections of letters
- focus on developing an ear for rhyme
- focus on letter identification
- focus on spelling patterns: *dr, fr, pr, tr*

Setup

- Gather your students together on the rug or at your class meeting place so that they will all be able to see the words of the poem.

- Have available a large piece of chart paper (and a writing implement), which you will be using over the course of a few sessions to create your own class "dream" poem.

Introduction

- Tell your students that after you read the poem through together, they will each get to add a line into a class list poem about dreams (focusing on the *dr* blend).

Interacting with the Text

- When you have read the poem through together, tell your students that they can each think of a line to add to a class list poem in which each line begins with the phrase "I dream." Tell them that their line can focus on a dream that happens in the night or the kind of dreaming that is more like a hope or a wish for the future. You may want to model several ideas for them first and remind them that the speaker in the poem is dreaming about riding a flying dragon.

- Call on individuals to tell you their "dream" line. As the students say a line, add it to your list poem. Remind them that each line must start with the words *I dream*. If any of the other blends appearing in the poem come up (for example, if a student suggests "I dream I am a *tree*"), draw your students' attention to them if they don't notice the blends themselves.

- Continue for as long as seems reasonable. You may need several sessions to complete the poem. Make sure to read it out loud! It is also nice to type up and keep a collection of poems the class writes together.

It can feel like a balancing act sometimes to guide your students' eyes by pointing below the words, read along yourself, and pay attention to each child's reaction and response to the poem at the same time. I now have the benefit of being able to watch my students in a way that I never did as a classroom teacher alone. Team teaching provides a wonderful opportunity to study students' reactions in a focused and removed way. When my teaching partner, Andrea, is doing the shared reading lesson, I have the luxury of not just noticing briefly but really studying and taking notes on who is reading eagerly and who seems timid, who is belting it out and who is playing with shoes, buttons, and so on. Because of this very different kind of looking, I find I am much quicker to notice the quieter children who are not diving into the shared reading process with as much enthusiasm as the rest of the class—and to move beyond that into speculating why this might be the case for each child. Some children are initially shy. Some might be overwhelmed by too much oral language. Some are busily thinking about other things, telling themselves stories in their heads, involved in the business of being six (or five, or seven, or eight!). Some may be sleepy. Some may be intimidated by the process. Through paying attention to my students during a time when I am not "on" myself, I find that I am much more effective at figuring out strategies to encourage more participation that fit each child.

Of course, many of us do not have the experience of team teaching. However, finding a colleague to do a trade with so that each of you comes in and watches the other's kids during shared reading and notes down who is reading and who is not can be extremely helpful. I wish I had done this when I was a teacher alone!

Extending Your Class' Work with "Dream"

- After you've written a class "dream" poem, ask students to write their own. You may want to ask them to try to use (or perhaps just to notice) *dr, fr, pr,* and *tr* words in their poems.

- Create individual word sorts for the blends *dr, fr, pr,* and *tr* that children may use on their own.

The Window Pane

Spelling patterns: long *a*: *a–e*
Sight words: *a, all, an, and, as, ever, go, going, it, just, like, my, on, the, then, will*

The Window Pane

On the window pane,
water drips.
Oh, will it ever wane?

Looks like
a horse's mane,
looks like
a twisting lane,
striped as a candy cane,
slick as an airplane.

The dripping and dripping
and inside all day.
Oh my, I'm going insane!

Then go outside, Mom says.
Go on! Go play! It's just rain!
　　　　　—Nicole Callihan

Curricular Goals for "The Window Pane"

Following is a list of possible curricular goals to be accomplished with this poem. You need not spend a lesson on each goal. Devote your lessons to meeting those curricular goals that will best serve your particular class.

- introductory work
- focus on comprehension
- building confidence and community
- focus on developing an ear for rhyme

- ■ focus on letter identification
- ■ focus on spelling patterns
- ■ focus on sight words

Poems in the Pocket Chart: A Lesson Using "The Window Pane"

Primary Curricular Goals

- ■ focus on comprehension
- ■ focus on spelling patterns
- ■ focus on sight words

Previously Covered

- ■ introductory work
- ■ focus on comprehension
- ■ building confidence and community
- ■ focus on developing an ear for rhyme
- ■ focus on spelling patterns
- ■ focus on sight words

Setup

- ■ You'll need a pocket chart for this activity; the longer charts designed for schedule cards are best for this poem, as it has fourteen lines. It should be hung in a place that the students can see and reach. You'll also need to write the poem up line by line on cards—sentence strips work great—that the children will be organizing on the chart.

- ■ Gather your students together on the rug or at your class meeting place so that they will all be able to see the words of the poem.

Introduction

- ■ Tell your students that after you read the poem through once, you'll be using the pocket chart to organize the lines. Make sure that they can also see the chart where you've written up the poem as they do this activity.

Interacting with the Text

- ■ When you have read the poem once through, tell your students that you'll be inviting individuals up to help sort out all of the lines of Nicole's poem, which you have written on cards, by putting them in order in the pocket chart.

- ■ Model for your students: Look at the first line of the poem, "On the window pane." Then show them how you look carefully through your collection of cards to find that line, and place it in the top pocket.

- ■ Ask your students what line should be found next. Invite an individual up to look through the lines and place the second line in the second pocket. Continue until the poem is finished.

■ Read through the poem again, this time using the pocket chart.

■ You may want to make this activity available to children during center time or some other activity time during the day so that they can practice in small groups.

From the Classroom: Individual Line-Sorting Activity

As with group word-sort activities, children will thoroughly enjoy having the opportunity to do the same work on their own. Tim chose to make the pocket chart available to his kids so that they could sort the poem's lines out on their own during center time, but he wanted more children to be able to practice this important work. He found that many children were motivated by the poems the class had been working with and that they provided a great opportunity for reading practice that some children resisted in other contexts. He decided to make miniature versions of the line-sorting materials, using paper, scissors, and glue. He typed Nicole's poem "The Window Pane" up in large font on one sheet of paper and formatted the paper so that there was a dotted line (for cutting) in between each line of the poem. He asked his students to cut the lines of the poem apart from each other and then to arrange them in order and glue them down on a piece of construction paper. He provided his class with copies of the poem to refer to as they arranged the poem's lines. He knew that children could theoretically just cut and glue the poem down line by line, but he also knew that they were doing important reading work anyway: reading the poem and checking their progress with the master copy multiple times throughout the process. Tim chose to do this activity with a small group during center time, but it could be done as a whole-class activity as well. The sheet Tim gave his students is in Figure 2–15.

Extending Your Class' Work with "The Window Pane"

■ Make a chart of all of the different ways children can think of to make the long *a* sound in words. You are, of course, focusing on long *a* with magic *e* in this poem, but children will no doubt recognize other words that have the long *a* sound that are spelled differently, using the vowel digraph or "vowel team" *ai: rain* or *brain*, for example.

The Window Pane

✂ -

On the window pane,

✂ -

water drips.

✂ -

Oh, will it ever wane?

✂ -

Looks like

✂ -

a horse's mane,

✂ -

looks like

✂ -

a twisting lane,

✂ -

striped as a candy cane,

✂ -

slick as an airplane.

✂ -

The dripping and dripping

✂ -

and inside all day.

✂ -

Oh my, I'm going insane!

✂ -

Then go outside, Mom says.

✂ -

Go on! Go play! It's just rain!

Figure 2–15 *"The Window Pane" line-sorting activity*

Microscope

Spelling patterns: long *o*: *o–e*
Sight words: *a, and, are, at, from, have, I, just, look, me, my, of, them, this, up, what, will*

> **Microscope**
> I hope, I hope
> my microscope
> will show me stones
> from way up close.
> This small black stone
> is nothing much
> just sitting on the ground.
> When I put it under the microscope:
> just look what I have found!
> A mountain, a slope,
> a bone, a rope
> of dark and shiny gems.
> Stones are like little planets
> if you look close enough at them.

Curricular Goals for "Microscope"

Following is a list of possible curricular goals to be accomplished with this poem. You need not spend a lesson on each goal. Devote your lessons to meeting those curricular goals that will best serve your particular class.

- introductory work
- focus on comprehension
- building confidence and community
- focus on directionality
- focus on words as discrete collections of letters
- focus on developing an ear for rhyme

■ focus on letter identification
■ focus on spelling patterns
■ focus on sight words

Kids Use the Pointer: A Lesson Using "Microscope"

Primary Curricular Goals

■ building confidence and community
■ focus on directionality
■ focus on words as discrete collections of letters

Previously Covered

■ introductory work
■ focus on comprehension

Setup

■ Gather your students together on the rug or at your class meeting place so that they will all be able to see the words of the poem.
■ Have your pointer available!

Introduction

■ Tell your students that after they read the poem through together as a class with you pointing below the words, they are going to take turns being the teacher and using the pointer to point below the words as the class reads along with them.

Interacting with the Text

■ Read through the poem once together, asking children to follow with their voices and their eyes.

■ Ask for volunteers to come and point below the words as the class follows along. Even children who are not able to decode all of the words in the poem (which may be many of your students) will enjoy this. At this point, the children have an understanding of directionality and words versus letters that will allow them to do this job even if they are unsure of some of the words. They will love being in front of the class and using the pointer (especially if it is fancy or sparkly in some way!).

■ Call on two or three children to use the pointer as the class reads along.

■ You may choose to repeat this activity throughout the day or during other shared reading sessions to accommodate all of those children who want to try it.

Extending Your Class' Work with "Microscope"

▪ Ask your students to imagine what stones look like under the microscope. Then ask them to draw a picture of what a regular old stone would look like way up close.

▪ If your class has access to a microscope (the kind that attaches to a computer is best, so that children can all see what the microscope sees), actually show your students what different kinds of stones look like under the microscope. How were the actual images different from what they imagined?

Five Mice

Spelling patterns: long *i: i–e*

Sight words: *a, an, and, before, but, could, down, fine, he, his, how, in, into, is, most, nice, not, now, of, one, or, our, she, so, some, than, that, the, then, they, to, where*

> *Five Mice*
>
> Five tiny mice, how they love to hide
> from Ike, our grouchy cat.
> Two mice find a fine place to hide
> right under a wide-brimmed hat.
>
> Ike opens his eyes and sniffs once or twice
> then rolls back into the sun
> He liked to chase mice, but now that he's old
> he'd rather lie down than run.
>
> One of the mice doesn't think twice.
> He hides right next to some fruit.
> He nibbles a peach, fuzzy and ripe.
> Then runs into an old boot.
>
> The fourth of the mice waits quite a while
> before she decides where to hide.
> Then she jets herself close to a hole
> And wiggles herself inside.
>
> The last of the mice, mouse number five,
> Is not so wily and fast
> In games and in races, most of the time
> This tiny old mouse comes in last.

He knows that he can't outrun a cat,
But he is so kind and wise,
He figures Ike and he could be friends
And strike a nice compromise.

So he tells grouchy Ike a funny joke
And gets the big cat to laugh
Then mouse number five shares his fine cheese
With his new friend—half and half.
—*Elizabeth Heisner*

Curricular Goals for "Five Mice"

Following is a list of possible curricular goals to be accomplished with this poem. You need not spend a lesson on each goal. Devote your lessons to meeting those curricular goals that will best serve your particular class.

- introductory work
- focus on comprehension
- building confidence and community
- focus on developing an ear for rhyme
- focus on letter identification
- focus on spelling patterns
- focus on sight words

Dramatizing a Poem: A Lesson Using "Five Mice"

Primary Curricular Goals

- building confidence and community

Previously Covered

- introductory work
- focus on comprehension

Setup

- Before teaching this lesson, you will want to have studied this poem enough so that many students are able to read it without adult support.
- Gather your students together on the rug or at your class meeting place so that they will all be able to see the words of the poem.
- Have your students sit in a circle or half circle rather than a clump so that there is space for children to act out the poem.

■ If you think your students could use the support, have each stanza of the poem written separately on a piece of paper and labeled by number for each of the chosen student readers to hold.

Introduction

■ Tell your students that today after reading the poem once through together, six children will each read a stanza of the poem as six other children act out the story of Ike and the five mice. Tell your students that you'll be doing this again so that everyone will eventually have a turn to participate.

Interacting with the Text

■ Read the poem through once with your class, making sure to highlight any of the teaching points you've recently been working on.
■ Choose six student volunteers to each read a stanza of the poem. Choose six student volunteers to act out the parts of the five mice and Ike the cat. Arrange the remaining children in a half circle or another comfortable audience arrangement.
■ Have the readers read the stanzas in succession as the actors act out the words of the poem. Remember, this is more about the process of reading and acting the poem's words than it is about performance—feel free to interrupt with prompts and reminders!
■ If you'd like, you can repeat immediately with another group of actors and readers, or you can wait until another day's lesson.

Extending Your Class' Work with "Five Mice"

■ Have your students illustrate the poem in storyboard fashion. The poem has a clear sequence, and providing them with a six-part template can help clarify their illustrations and their understanding of the poem.

CHAPTER THREE

Deeper In

Children moving into this phase of shared reading, while most often having discovered the joy of reading independently, still thoroughly enjoy and benefit from reading together as a community. The poems in this section highlight more sophisticated word patterns, such as vowel digraphs (or vowel teams), silent beginning consonants, and triple-letter blends. Children will also be able to investigate hard and soft *c* and *g*. The poems also feature simple homophones and contractions as well as an introduction to compound words.

■ Sight Words Appearing in This Chapter's Poems

a, all, also, am, an, and, anything, are, around, as, at, be, beautiful, between, but, by, came, can, can't, could, don't, down, everything, even, ever, from, for, full, get, go, good, had, has, have, he, her, here, his, house, I, if, in, into, is, isn't, it, it's, just, like, little, love, may, me, more, much, must, my, no, not, of, on, only, other, out, said, same, saw, say, see, seen, set, she, she's, so, some, somebody, something, than, that, the, their, them, then, there, these, they, this, through, to, too, two, until, up, use, want, was, went, were, when, where, which, who, will, with, yes, you, your, you've

■ Spelling Patterns and Other Features Appearing in This Chapter's Poems

Vowel digraphs: *ai, ea, ee, oa, oo*
Silent beginning consonants: *kn, wr*
Triple-letter blends: *scr, spr, str*
Homophones: *be, bee; hair, hare; tail, tale; to, too, two*
Hard and soft *c* and *g*
Contractions: *couldn't, didn't, don't, he'll, I'll, isn't, let's, she'll, she's, we'll, we've, won't, you'll*
Compound words: *afternoon, anything, awestruck, beehives, buttercup, butterflies, downpour, heartbeat, ladybugs, lopsided, moonbeam, postcard, rosebud, seashores, sideways, somebody, someplace, something, starlight, sunflowers, sunrise, sweetheart, wheelbarrow, wishbone*

■ Mining the Poems for Teaching Points: Curricular Goals Associated with More Advanced Shared Reading Work

While the curricular goals are introduced in a sequence that many teachers might choose to follow, the sequence is certainly not set in stone. You might choose to focus on sight words before focusing on spelling patterns, for example, or you might choose not to spend time on sight words at all from a particular poem. You also might focus a couple of lessons on the same curricular goal, especially if your students seem to need more time. Pick and choose what makes sense for *your* class.

Introductory Work

Children at this stage of shared reading are developing great independence as readers. You may find that your students are reading within a wide range of levels. Some may be reading and comprehending sophisticated chapter books. Some may be reading less sophisticated texts and struggling to read fluently. For some children, reading develops naturally and seemingly effortlessly. For others, it is clear to us (and to them) that it is a tremendous amount of hard work. Shared reading with poetry is appropriate and useful to all children, no matter their reading level. When you introduce a new poem at this stage, you may find that they will more readily notice more sophisticated word work on their own. They will also be able to discuss a poem's meaning in more sophisticated terms, and their understanding of poetry's figurative language is continuing to develop. It continues to be important to spend time getting to know a poem before diving into the word work you have planned. Deepening comprehension for all children will only support the work you plan to do later on.

Focus on Comprehension

Just as in the previous stage, you may find that you need not devote an entire lesson to comprehension as you may have done earlier on in the shared reading process. You might feel that you have adequately addressed issues of comprehension during your introductory day. You may, however, choose to enhance comprehension by spending some more time throughout the process doing activities or projects based around comprehension. Illustrating poems, acting them out, and writing class poems based on the shared reading poem are all ways that you can build on your students' comprehension at this point. You will also be able to spend more time unpacking the figurative language in poetry during this stage, and you might want to enhance students' comprehension by asking them to write their own poems using figurative language, inspired by shared reading poems.

Building Confidence and Community

Just as in the early stages, reading together lifts the spirits, fills the heart, and centers and connects a group of people. This is no less important at this more advanced stage! Children who may struggle to read fluently on their own will also take comfort in reading together and will be able to take risks and try things out that they may not feel comfortable doing alone. The support of the group will encourage and lift the individual, and the group is made stronger by the blend of individual voices.

Focus on Developing an Ear for Rhyme

Rhyme continues to engage children at this stage—and indeed it engages people of all ages! Looking for and generating rhymes bring a playful tone to this work. Children will be more able to notice and articulate how the way words are made affects the way they sound. They will also be able to begin comparing words that rhyme yet are made with *different* spelling patterns—*rain* and *cane*, for example—as their bank of known spelling patterns develops. Work with simple homophones will extend that conversation as well.

Focus on Spelling Patterns

Children at this phase of shared reading are ready to puzzle over vowel digraphs that make up CVVC words. You'll introduce silent beginning letters in *wr* and *kn*. Children will be ready for triple-letter consonant blends as well. They will be ready for (and very curious about) the more sophisticated word work to be done with homophones, contractions, and compound words. As with all shared reading work, you will be able to differentiate instruction for your students relatively easily by asking them to interact with the text in ways that lift the level of their thinking, no matter where they are starting from.

Focus on Sight Words

Children at this stage have developed a large bank of sight words that they are able to identify in their reading and use in their writing. You may choose to use shared reading poems as a way to introduce new sight words to your students. You might also want to use the poems as a way for students to review sight words they are getting to know. You can extend the sight word work provided by a shared reading poem by incorporating those words into familiar sight word games and activities you may already be playing with your class as well.

The Poems

"The Ice Cream Scream," by Nicole Callihan
  poem containing the spelling pattern *ea*
  sight words: *a, all, and, at, for, get, I, me, my, only, said, she, the, then, want, was, who, you, your*

"Sky House"
  poem containing the spelling pattern *oo*
  sight words: *and, everything, from, house, in, is, out, the, to*

"Tree"
  poem containing the spelling patterns *ea, ee*
  sight words: *an, and, between, for, if, is, it's, my, on, see, the, their, they, to, yes*

"Hurricane Train"
  poem containing the spelling patterns *ai* and *a–e*
  sight words: *a, and, as, down, just, the, through, up, we, were*

"CAT/BIRD," by Judy Katz
>   poem containing the spelling pattern *oa*
>   sight words: *a, and, but, can't, has, have, her, in, seen, she, she's, the, to, with, you*

"Knight"
>   poem containing the silent beginning consonants *kn*
>   sight words: *a, and, had, he, his, in, it, must, on, set, some, the, then, to, until*

"Read (Don't Wread)," by Amy Ludwig VanDerwater
>   poem containing the silent beginning consonants *wr*
>   sight words: *a, and, at, don't, in, which, with, you, your*

"Spring Surprise"
>   poem containing the triple-letter blends *scr, spr, str*
>   sight words: *a, and, but, can, get, had, I, in, into, my, not, other, saw, so, the, them, then, there, these, to, use, was, were, when*

"The Golden Giraffe and the Cinnamon Cat"
>   poem containing soft and hard *c*, soft and hard *g*
>   sight words: *a, all, and, around, came, his, I, in, little, on, out, saw, she, the, then, to, went, when, with*

"2" by Amy Ludwig VanDerwater
>   poem containing the homophones *to, too, two*
>   sight words: *also, and, are, but, by, for, go, good, is, isn't, it, it's, just, like, may, more, much, same, than, that, the, them, they, she, so, to, too, two, up, when, where, will, you, your, you've*

"A Tall Tale"
>   poem containing the homophones *be, bee; hair, hare; tail, tale*
>   sight words: *a, and, as, at, be, beautiful, for, from, he, his, I'll, in, just, little, not, of, so, the, was*

"The Cake Isn't for Us!"
>   poem containing the contractions *couldn't, didn't, don't, he'll, I'll, isn't, let's, she'll, she's, we'll, we've, won't, you'll*
>   sight words: *and, even, ever, if, it, just, no, out, say, she, so, the, there, we, when, will, you*

"Postcard from Someplace Lopsided," by Nicole Callihan
>   poem containing compound words: *afternoon, anything, awestruck, beehives, buttercup, butterflies, downpour, heartbeat, ladybugs, lopsided, moonbeam, postcard, rosebud, seashores, sideways, somebody, someplace, something, starlight, sunflowers, sunrise, sweetheart, wheelbarrow, wishbone*
>   sight words: *a, all, am, and, anything, be, but, could, do, from, full, have, here, I, I'd, in, is, it, just, love, my, of, on, see, so, somebody, something, the, this, to, you*

The Ice Cream Scream

Spelling pattern: *ea*
Sight words: *a, all, and, at, for, get, I, me, my, only, said, she, the, then, want, was,
who, you, your*

> ### The Ice Cream Scream
> I was screaming
> and screaming
> for ice cream.
> I screamed.
> You screamed.
> Mom gave me a bean.
> *A bean?* I said.
> *Who wants a bean!*
> *I want ice cream!*
> She looked at my nails
> (unclean!).
> She looked at my head
> (all dreams!).
> *Finish your bean,* Mom said,
> *and then, only then,*
> *you may get your ice cream.*
> —Nicole Callihan

Curricular Goals for "The Ice Cream Scream"

Following is a list of possible curricular goals to be accomplished with this poem.
You need not spend a lesson on each goal. Devote your lessons to meeting those
curricular goals that will best serve your particular class.

- introductory work
- focus on comprehension

■ building confidence and community
■ focus on developing an ear for rhyme
■ focus on spelling patterns
■ focus on sight words

Adding in ea: A Lesson Using "The Ice Cream Scream"

Primary Curricular Goals

■ focus on spelling pattern: vowel digraph *ea*

Previously Covered

■ introductory work
■ focus on comprehension
■ building confidence and community

Setup

■ Before the lesson, cover up several instances of the appearance of the vowel digraph *ea* in the poem with sticky notes or label tape.
■ Gather your students together on the rug or at your class meeting place so that they will all be able to see the words of the poem.
■ Have your pointer and a marker available.

Introduction

■ Tell your students that after you read through the poem together, you are going to be paying attention to the words that contain the vowel digraph (you may choose to call these *vowel teams*) *ea*. Remind them of any work you have previously done to notice or otherwise mark these words in the poem.

Interacting with the Text

■ Read the poem through together. Children will notice that some of the words have a missing piece!

■ Pointing to one of the words you've covered up, ask students to guess what word it is. When they have guessed the word, ask them to guess what two letters need to be filled in so that the word is complete.

■ Ask a volunteer to come and add the *ea*.

■ Continue until each of the words missing *ea* has been filled in.

■ Read the poem through together once more.

■ Ask students to volunteer to read the poem aloud to the class, paying particular attention to the dialogue. This poem provides a great opportunity for children to practice reading with expression.

■ Ask students to each draw a self-portrait imagining what they might look like if offered a bean instead of ice cream!

Sky House

Spelling pattern: *oo*
Sight words: *and, everything, from, house, in, is, out, the, to*

> ### *Sky House*
> The sky is the clouds' blue house.
> Clouds roam from room to room.
> Birds zoom in and out the windows.
> The cool wind is everything breathing.

Curricular Goals for "Sky House"

Following is a list of possible curricular goals to be accomplished with this poem. You need not spend a lesson on each goal. Devote your lessons to meeting those curricular goals that will best serve your particular class.

- introductory work
- focus on comprehension
- building confidence and community
- focus on developing an ear for rhyme
- focus on spelling patterns
- focus on sight words

Draw Your Own Sky House: A Lesson Using "Sky House"

Primary Curricular Goals

- focus on comprehension

Previously Covered

- introductory work

Setup

- Gather your students together on the rug or at your class meeting place so that they will all be able to see the words of the poem.
- Have paper and drawing materials available.

Introduction

■ Tell your students that after you finish reading the poem through together, they'll be discussing what it means, and then each of them will draw an illustration that will show how they imagine the world of the poem.

Interacting with the Text

■ Read the poem through together.

■ Ask your students to tell you what they notice about the poem. They may choose to highlight word-based or meaning-based information.

■ Ask your class to consider the comparison in the poem—to what is the sky being compared? To what is the wind being compared? You may ask your students to elaborate with you on the metaphor of sky as house. You could ask things like, "If the sky is the clouds' house, what do the clouds think of all of those airplanes passing through?"

■ Tell your students that they will be able to illustrate the poem, using their imaginations to create their own sky houses. Have them close their eyes for several seconds to visualize what they'll draw. You may want to have several children share their ideas before they go off to work.

From the Classroom: Fleshing Out a Comprehension Conversation about Metaphor

Roger's class of second graders has just started working with the poem "Sky House." They are comfortable reading the poem through together. Because the poem is based on a very visual metaphor, Roger wants to spend some time discussing the poem's meaning before his next series of lessons, which will focus on the spelling pattern *oo*. He wants to see what the kids are picking up on first, and then he hopes to turn the conversation in the direction of unpacking the metaphor (or as his class calls it, comparison). He knows that he'll be asking children to illustrate the poem later on, and he wants to make sure that everyone has a good grasp on how the poem works first.

"So, everyone, I'm wondering what you notice about 'Sky House.' It's a little different from some of the poems we've been reading lately, isn't it? Carl?"

Carl, a thoughtful boy with perpetually messy hair, says, "Well, it doesn't rhyme like most of the other ones."

"*Room* and *zoom* rhyme," points out Kevin.

"True, Kevin," Roger says. "But I see what you're noticing too, Carl; there are rhyming words inside the poem, but the poem itself isn't built around a rhyme scheme. I mean, the rhyming words don't come at the end of the line like they often do in rhyming poems. What else are we noticing? Talia?"

"I think it says that the sky is like a house, and the clouds are living in it like people do!"

"Interesting," Roger says. "Take a look at what these cloud people are doing in the poem. Shania?"

Shania says, "They're going around in the house, going from room to room."

"Shania, why do you suppose the poet had the clouds doing that, going from room to room?" Robert sees that Shania hasn't quite understood his question, so he rephrases. "How do real clouds move around in the sky?"

"They float around. Oh! Maybe the clouds are roaming from room to room because real clouds kind of float around like that."

"Makes sense to me! How about the birds, what are they doing? Talia?"

"They zoom in and out the window, but the sky doesn't really have any windows."

"Well, that's the great thing about poems, isn't it?"

Roger and his class continue discussing the poem for a few more moments until he's satisfied that they all have an understanding of the poem's metaphor.

Extending Your Class' Work with "Sky House"

- Ask students to create their own extended metaphor based on "Sky House." If the sky is the house for the clouds, what is the moon? What is the forest? What are the stars? You may choose to ask children to turn their comparisons into their own poems.

- After having students illustrate the poem, make a "Sky House" bulletin board using all of their illustrations. You may want to post the poem as well. Alternatively, you could have children write their own extended metaphor poems and then illustrate them, and then create a bulletin board out of those.

Tree

Spelling patterns: *ea, ee*
Sight words: *an, and, between, for, if, is, it's, my, on, see, the, their, they, to, yes*

> **Tree**
> The tree
> is an umbrella
> for the birds
> on my block.
> They peer
> between leaves
> to see
> if it's stopped.
> Yes!
> They flee,
> and leave
> their green umbrella
> dripping.

Curricular Goals for "Tree"

Following is a list of possible curricular goals to be accomplished with this poem. You need not spend a lesson on each goal. Devote your lessons to meeting those curricular goals that will best serve your particular class.

- introductory work
- focus on comprehension
- building confidence and community
- focus on developing an ear for rhyme
- focus on spelling patterns
- focus on sight words

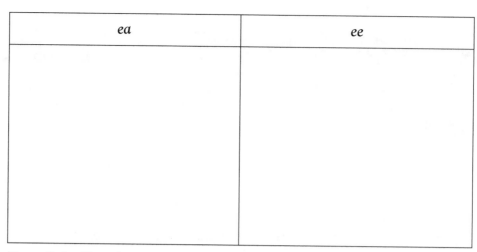

ea	*ee*

Figure 3–1   Chart for sorting *ea* and *ee* words

Which /e/ Is It? A Lesson Using "Tree"

Primary Curricular Goals

- focus on spelling pattern: vowel digraph *ee*

Previously Covered

- focus on comprehension
- building confidence and community

Setup

- Gather your students together on the rug or at your class meeting place so that they will all be able to see the words of the poem.
- Have a chart available with two columns, one labeled *ea*, and one labeled *ee* (see Figure 3–1.)
- Have a writing implement available.

Introduction

- Tell your students that after you read the poem once through together, you'll be paying attention to the words with the vowel digraph *ee* that appear in the poem and then making a chart that will help them keep track of which words use *ee* to make the long *e* sound, and which words use *ea*.

Interacting with the Text

- Ask your students to read the poem with you.

- Ask children to notice which words in the poem use the vowel digraph *ee* to make the long *e* sound. Call on several children to say a word or two out loud.

- Ask your students if there are any words in the poem that use a different vowel digraph to make the long *e* sound (they will notice *ea* in *leave* and *leaves*).

- Tell your students that you'll be adding words to the chart you've made to help them keep track of which is which. Ask volunteers to come up and write the *ea* and *ee* words in the appropriate columns.

- If you have time, ask children to brainstorm more words to add to each column. Keep the chart posted in the room so that children can see it.

From the Classroom: Using Word Charts Throughout the Day

Helen's class has been collecting a chart of words containing either *ea* or *ee* during shared reading time. She's hung the chart on the rope that crosses the classroom so that children can see it from their writing seats. Helen is conferring with a student, Henry, about his personal narrative. Henry is working on editing his piece, which is about a recent soccer game. As Helen looks over Henry's shoulder, she notices that he's spelled the word *team* as *teem*. She knows that this word has been added to the *ea* side of the chart and decides to remind him to check the chart as he is editing.

"Henry, I just noticed something. Remember the chart we've been adding to during shared reading time? I think it'll help you as you're editing. Look at this word, *teem*. Do you see anything on the chart that will help you check that word out?"

Henry looks up to the chart; Helen can see him scanning the lists. As he comes to the word *team*, he says, "Oh yeah!" and immediately makes the change. After finishing up with Henry, Helen decides to remind the whole class quickly about using the chart to help them with editing.

"Everyone, look up for a minute. When I was meeting with Henry, I remembered something that I want to remind you all about: you can use the *ea/ee* chart we've been making during shared reading time to help you check out words you're not sure of. Henry just found the word *team* up there and he was able to make a change as he edited. If you're editing, too, you might want to check out your *ea* and *ee* words with our chart. OK, you can keep on writing!"

Extending Your Class' Work with "Tree"

- This poem is a good one to dramatize because you can have half the class sit in a circle and be the umbrella while the rest of the class is in the center of the circle as the sheltered birds. As the sun comes out in the poem, the "birds" can take a step outside the circle and "fly" away!

- Have your students illustrate the poem.

- I always like reading poems that fit with the weather or other events of the day. Rainy days especially are good days for rain poems; if you like to read rain poems to your class on rainy days, this is a good one to keep on hand.

Hurricane Train

Spelling patterns: *ai, a–e*
Sight words: *a, and, as, down, just, the, through, up, we, were*

> ### *Hurricane Train*
> We rode the train
> through the hurricane.
> Raindrops flew down
> the windowpanes.
> The train rocked back and forth
> as the wind blew up a gale,
> but we were safe inside,
> just sailing down the rails.

Curricular Goals for "Hurricane Train"

Following is a list of possible curricular goals to be accomplished with this poem. You need not spend a lesson on each goal. Devote your lessons to meeting those curricular goals that will best serve your particular class.

- introductory work
- focus on comprehension
- building confidence and community
- focus on developing an ear for rhyme
- focus on spelling patterns
- focus on sight words

Is It ai *or* a *and Magic* e? A Lesson Using "Hurricane Train"

Primary Curricular Goals

- focus on spelling patterns: *ai* versus *a–e*

Previously Covered

- introductory work
- focus on comprehension
- building confidence and community
- focus on developing an ear for rhyme
- focus on spelling pattern: *ai* versus *a–e*

Setup

- You will want to have spent time with your class during a previous lesson noticing and perhaps marking with different-colored transparent tape those words containing the long /a/ sound made by the vowel digraph *ai* and those words containing the long /a/ sound made with an *a* and the magic *e* at the end of the word.

- Before the lesson, print out a copy of the poem for each student, taking care to leave a space in place of each of the words containing long /a/ so that children will be able to fill it in later.

- Gather your students together on the rug or at your class meeting place so that they will all be able to see the words of the poem.

Introduction

- Tell your students that after you read the poem together, they'll have a chance to practice with the different ways to make the long /a/ sound on their own by filling in the missing words on their own copy of the poem.

Interacting with the Text

- Read the poem once through with your class. Before reading, ask the students to pay particular attention to the *ai* and *a–e* words in the poem.

- You may want to discuss with your students what they notice about these words before you invite them to fill in the missing words in their own poems.

- Before sending students off to their work seats with their copies of the poem to fill in, you may want to cover up the poem chart so that children can't refer to it. Or if you feel you want your students to have the extra support, keep the poem visible.

- You might want to have students work in partnerships in this endeavor so that they can support each other.

Extending Your Class' Work with "Hurricane Train"

■ Create and extend a class chart of *ai* and *a–e* words and post it in your room so that children can refer to it when they are reading and writing.

■ Have children make up silly sentences using as many *ai* words as possible. You may ask them to illustrate these silly sentences. (See Figure 3–2.)

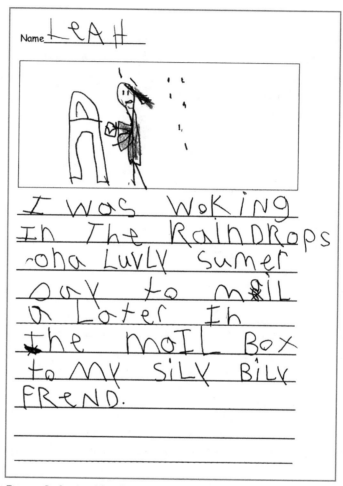

Figure 3–2 *Leah's silly sentence using* ai

CAT/BIRD

Spelling patterns: *oa*
Sight words: *a, and, but, can't, has, have, her, in, seen, she, she's, the, to, with, you*

> **CAT/BIRD**
> Have you seen the cat
> with the pretty black coat?
> She has a robin
> stuck in her throat.
> She can't meow
> but she's started to sing—
> And her pretty black coat
> has sprouted a wing.
> —*Judy Katz*

Curricular Goals for "CAT/BIRD"

Following is a list of possible curricular goals to be accomplished with this poem. You need not spend a lesson on each goal. Devote your lessons to meeting those curricular goals that will best serve your particular class.

- introductory work
- focus on comprehension
- building confidence and community
- focus on developing an ear for rhyme
- focus on spelling patterns
- focus on sight words

Writing Your Own Poems Using oa: A Lesson Using "CAT/BIRD"

Primary Curricular Goals

- focus on spelling pattern: *oa*

Previously Covered

- introductory work
- focus on comprehension
- building confidence and community
- focus on developing an ear for rhyme
- focus on spelling pattern: *oa*

Setup

- Gather your students together on the rug or at your class meeting place so that they will all be able to see the words of the poem.
- Have writing paper and chart paper for listing words available.

Introduction

- Tell your students that after you've read the poem through together, the class will be brainstorming a list of words that contain the vowel digraph *ea* and then each student will write a poem of her own that uses those words (you may choose to do this lesson as a continuation of a previous lesson in which you have already generated a list of words containing *oa*; if that is the case, skip that part of the following lesson).

Interacting with the Text

- Read the poem once through with your class. Tell the kids to keep their eyes open for words containing the vowel digraph *oa*.

- Generate a list of words that contain *oa*, both from within Judy's poem and other words children think of.

- Tell children that they will be able to choose from the list or from other *oa* words they can think of to make a short poem on their own. Depending on your class' comfort with independent writing, you may or may not want to model for them or to create the beginning of a poem together before they go off. For example, you may have the words *oat*, *moat*, *coat*, and *boat* in your list. You could suggest the first two lines, "A horse stepped into a little boat / to sail across the castle's moat," and then ask children to volunteer to fill in another line and another line.

- When you feel that your children are comfortable with the assignment, send them off to create their own poems using *oa*. If your students are not comfortable doing this on their own, you may end the lesson instead with a poem coconstructed by the large group.

From the Classroom: How to Coconstruct a Poem with Your Class

Jane and her class have busily been collecting *oa* words, both from Judy's poem and from their own heads. They've got a good list now, and Jane thinks they're ready to try building a poem together. The list they've collected is as follows:

oa **Words**

> coat
> throat
> boat
> moat
> oat
> float
> goat

Jane would eventually like to have her students write their own *oa* poems, but she wants to try one together first. She asks her second graders to listen as she reads through the list because they'll be using the words on the list to start their own poem. After reading the list, she asks a brave soul to think of a first line and then calls on Marcus.

"Marcus, would you like to start us off? What's your idea?"

"Well, how about . . . 'The goat had a sore throat'?"

The class giggles. "Sound good, everyone?" Jane asks before writing Marcus' line at the top of the chart paper. She reads the line aloud as she writes and then asks if someone has another line he or she would like to add. "Remember to use at least one of our *oa* words in your line! Betsy?"

"How about 'He had a sore throat 'cause he ate too much oats,'" announces Betsy, with pride.

The class erupts in giggles again. Jane knows that this is not likely to be a quiet class activity—playing with rhyming words almost always makes students laugh! She writes Betsy's line below Marcus' line (making sure to ask Betsy if it's OK that she change "too much" to "too many") and then reads the couplet to the class: "The goat had a sore throat. / He had a sore throat because he ate too many oats."

"What's next, everyone? We haven't used the word *boat* yet or *coat*. Theo?"

"'He got cold and he put on his coat . . . in the boat,'" Theo says, to more laughter from the class.

"How about just the coat part . . . 'He got cold so he put on his coat.' Sound OK, Theo? Everyone?"

Jane continues eliciting lines from the class, gently steering them toward correct grammar when they are a bit off, and toward sense when they suggest lines without meaning. By the end of the session, the class has written the following poem:

The goat had a sore throat.

He had a sore throat because he ate too many oats.

He got cold so he put on his coat.

He saw his friend across the moat.

He floated over in his little boat.

He was glad to see his friend and he forgot about his throat.

Not a work of art, perhaps, but the activity certainly helps children practice with the long /o/ sound!

Extending Your Class' Work with "CAT/BIRD"

■ This is an awfully silly one to illustrate! Children will enjoy drawing little cats with wings sticking out.

Knight

Spelling patterns: *kn*
Sight words: *a, and, had, he, his, in, it, must, on, set, some, the, then, to, until*

> **Knight**
> The fighting knight
> knocked a knuckle
> on his shield.
> He knew he must rest
> until it had healed.
> He reached in his knapsack
> and set his yarn on his knee,
> then decided to knit
> and drink some tea.

Curricular Goals for "Knight"

Following is a list of possible curricular goals to be accomplished with this poem. You need not spend a lesson on each goal. Devote your lessons to meeting those curricular goals that will best serve your particular class.

- introductory work
- focus on comprehension
- building confidence and community
- focus on developing an ear for rhyme
- focus on spelling patterns
- focus on sight words

Acting Out the Poem: A Lesson Using "Knight"

Primary Curricular Goals

- focus on comprehension

Previously Covered

- ▪ introductory work

Setup

- ▪ Gather your students together on the rug or at your class meeting place so that they will all be able to see the words of the poem.

- ▪ You will need to ask the children to move into a circle at the edge of your meeting area after you have practiced reading the poem together a couple of times.

Introduction

- ▪ Tell your students that after you read through the poem together, individuals will have a chance to act out the poem as the class reads it aloud.

Interacting with the Text

- ▪ Read the poem once through with your class, pointing below the words. Ask your students to follow along with their eyes and voices as you read.

- ▪ After you've read the poem through, move your students into a circle. Hopefully they will still be able to see the words of the poem, though some of them might have to turn around to do so.

- ▪ Ask for a volunteer to act out the poem as the rest of the class reads the poem through. Remind the actor that her job is to show the poem's words with her body.

- ▪ Repeat several times. You may need to repeat this lesson again another day if you have lots of volunteers!

Extending Your Class' Work with "Knight"

- ▪ Using the *kn* words your class has collected on a chart, ask students to write their own silly sentences.

Read (Don't Wread)

Spelling pattern: *wr*
Sight words: *a, and, at, don't, in, which, with, you, your*

Read (Don't Wread)
Wring your hands.
Write a song.
Read a book.
Right a wrong.
Wiggle fingers.
Wriggle toes.
Wrestle in your
wrinkled clothes.

Ring a bell.
Wrap a box.
Watch a wren
escape a fox.
Twist a wrench
with your wrist.
Rack your brain.
Write a list.

Read
(don't wread)
and you'll succeed
at knowing
which *r* sound
you need.

Don't let
silent *w*
trouble you.
—Amy Ludwig VanDerwater

Curricular Goals for "Read (Don't Wread)"

Following is a list of possible curricular goals to be accomplished with this poem. You need not spend a lesson on each goal. Devote your lessons to meeting those curricular goals that will best serve your particular class.

- introductory work
- focus on comprehension
- building confidence and community
- focus on developing an ear for rhyme
- focus spelling pattern
- focus on sight words

Recognizing wr Words: A Lesson Using "Read (Don't Wread)"

Primary Curricular Goals

- focus on spelling pattern: *wr*

Previously Covered

- introductory work
- focus on comprehension
- building confidence and community
- focus on developing an ear for rhyme
- focus on spelling pattern: *wr*

Setup

- You will want to have already presented a lesson in which children were asked to notice and mark the words containing *wr* in the poem—they should be familiar with *wr*. The great thing about Amy's poem is that the poem itself refers to the spelling pattern, which helps children remember the way the spelling pattern works.

- Gather your students together on the rug or at your class meeting place so that they will all be able to see the words of the poem.

Introduction

- Tell your students that you'll be reading the poem through together, paying special attention to those words containing *wr*. Tell them that after you read the poem through, you'll be playing a guessing game about words with *wr*.

Interacting with the Text

- Read the poem once through with your class, pointing below the words. Ask your students to follow along with their eyes and voices as you read, paying attention to the *wr* words.

- After you've read the poem through, explain the game to your students. You'll be asking them to close their eyes. You'll be choosing a word in the poem that starts with the /r/ sound; it may use the *wr* spelling pattern and it may not. They need to think about the word and try to visualize it in their minds. If they think the word does start with *wr*, they'll raise their hands. After everyone has had a chance to think, you'll ask them to open their eyes and check their thoughts with the word in the poem. You may want to do a practice round in which kids can keep their eyes open.

■ Go through several words from the poem, making sure to provide examples of both *wr* words and *r* words.

■ Make sure to keep the tone lighthearted and fun!

From the Classroom: Tips for Inclusion—the Impulsive Child

Casey is a very verbal and enthusiastic second grader who is working on controlling impulsive behaviors on the rug. Earlier in the year, Casey found it nearly impossible to raise her hand and wait to be called on before speaking; she has made a lot of progress in that area, though it still takes her a great deal of extra effort to wait her turn and to stay settled on the rug. Bob, her teacher, is imagining that Casey might have a hard time playing the *wr* guessing game he's planned for this morning's shared reading activity. He knows that it will be hard for Casey to keep her eyes closed when he asks children to do so (so that they can raise their hands if they think the word he is saying begins with *wr*). He decides to give it a try first, but he's got an intervention in mind in the event that Casey does have a hard time keeping her eyes closed. After explaining the game to his students, Bob begins.

OK, everyone, get ready for the first word. Eyes closed. Everyone! Casey, eyes closed all the way. OK, the first word is the word *write*. If *write* starts with *wr*, raise your hands. No peeking!"

Casey is wiggling in her rug spot with her hands over her eyes. Bob can see that she is really trying not to peek, but after a moment, there are her brown eyes peering out between her fingers. Bob lets it go for the moment and waits until the rest of the students have decided whether or not to raise their hands. Everyone's hand has gone up—Bob chose the word *write* for the first example because he knows that all of the children are very familiar with that one from seeing it on the schedule every day.

"OK, eyes open, second graders. Check your answer with the poem—were you right?"

"Yes!" says the class.

Bob decides to employ the intervention he was imagining earlier; instead of designing an intervention specifically for Casey, he thought of a way to change the game's structure so that she (and probably others) would have an easier time staying within bounds.

"This time, guys, I'm going to actually cover up the whole poem. I'll just flip the chart over on the back side. This way you don't have to worry about keeping your eyes closed—I know that can be hard." He winks at Casey, who beams up at him. After flipping the chart over, he continues with the game. It works just as well for everyone; he simply flips the poem back to the front when he asks children to check their thinking.

Extending Your Class' Work with "Read (Don't Wread)"

■ Words containing *wr* must simply be memorized. Creating a chart and allowing children to add onto it when they come across a word in their independent reading or throughout the day will help them build a bank of *wr* words that they are familiar with and can refer to when they are writing.

■ Because this poem is full of action words, it great to have kids act out the poem or make gestures as they read.

■ You might want to ask a student (or do this yourself) to illustrate the poem on chart paper. Some of the words are tricky and might be unfamiliar to many children, so having little visual cues next to them might help students become more fluent with the poem. (See Figure 3–3.)

Figure 3–3 *An illustrated chart of "Read (Don't Wread)"*

Spring Surprise

Spelling patterns: triple-letter *r* blends *scr, spr, str*
Sight words: *a, and, but, can, get, had, I, in, into, my, not, other, saw, so, the, them, then, there, these, to, use, was, were, when*

Spring Surprise
I scrambled through the brambles
because I had lost my way.
I thought I was heading home,
but I was aimed the other way!
I strolled, I stretched, and then I scurried
(I was starting to get worried.)
The wind was getting stronger
and the path was looking longer
and then I felt a strange sensation
between my shoulder blades.
I scratched and scritched—
my shoulders itched.
My back was sprouting wings!
They were striped blue and gold.
I thought, "I can use these things."
I spread them wide and flapped them hard
and sprung into the air.
I saw my house, I saw my roof.
I knew I could get there.
I struggled and I strained
and I landed in the yard.
I've never gotten lost again—
when you fly, it's not so hard!

Curricular Goals for "Spring Surprise"

Following is a list of possible curricular goals to be accomplished with this poem. You need not spend a lesson on each goal. Devote your lessons to meeting those curricular goals that will best serve your particular class.

- introductory work
- focus on comprehension
- building confidence and community
- focus on developing an ear for rhyme
- focus in spelling patterns
- focus on sight words

Differentiating Between scr, spr, and str: A Lesson Using "Spring Surprise"

Primary Curricular Goals

- focus on spelling patterns: triple-letter *r* blends *scr*, *spr*, *str*

Previously Covered

- introductory work
- focus on comprehension
- building confidence and community
- focus on developing an ear for rhyme

Setup

- You will want the children to have had enough prior experience with this long poem that they can comfortably read along with you.

- Gather your students together on the rug or at your class meeting place so that they will all be able to see the words of the poem.

- Have your pointer available as well as materials for the children to use when marking the blends *scr*, *spr*, and *str* in the poem. You'll need three different colors that will visually differentiate the blends for the children; I prefer to use transparent colored tape for this because it's easy to see.

Introduction

- Tell your students that after you read the poem through together, you'll be paying special attention to the words that start with the blends *scr*, *spr*, and *str*. Tell them you'll be using different-colored tape to mark each of the three blends on the poem. (If you are limited by time or if your students would benefit from doing this more slowly, you may choose to divide this lesson into three parts and focus on just one of the three blends each day.)

Interacting with the Text

- Ask your students to read the poem with you.

■ Tell students that you'll be asking them to come up and help you mark the three blends you're focusing on in the poem, each in a different color. Model marking each of the blends for them in a different color so they have a key to refer to. For example, use blue tape to mark the *spr* in *spring*. Mark the *scr* in *scrambled* with yellow, and highlight the *str* in *strolled* with green.

■ You may choose to focus on one pattern at a time and ask children to notice and mark all of the *spr* words first, for example, and then move on to the others. If you ask children to notice and mark any of the blends, it brings another level of challenge to the activity, as they must distinguish between the three and choose the appropriate color. When you're finished, the poem will look something like this:

Spring Surprise

I scrambled through the brambles

because I had lost my way.

I thought I was heading home,

but I was aimed the other way!

I strolled, I stretched, and then I scurried

(I was starting to get worried.)

The wind was getting stronger

and the path was looking longer

and then I felt a strange sensation

between my shoulder blades.

I scratched and scritched—

my shoulders itched.

My back was sprouting wings!

They were striped blue and gold.

I thought, "I can use these things."

I spread them wide and flapped them hard

and sprung into the air.

I saw my house, I saw my roof.

I knew I could get there.

I struggled and I strained

and I landed in the yard.

I've never gotten lost again—

when you fly, it's not so hard!

Extending Your Class' Work with "Spring Surprise"

■ Ask your students to imagine what they would do if they suddenly sprouted wings. Then ask them each to write (and illustrate, if you like) a short creative writing piece about their adventures. This can be compiled into a great class collection and sent home or kept in the room. Children love to read each other's work!

Golden Giraffe and Cinnamon Cat

Letter sounds: soft and hard *c*, soft and hard *g*
Sight words: *a, all, and, around, came, his, I, in, little, on, out, saw, she, the, then, to, went, when, with*

> ### Golden Giraffe and Cinnamon Cat
> When I went to the circus
> I saw a cinnamon-colored cat
> cycling around the circle
> with a carrot in his hat.
>
> And then out came the giraffe
> in a gown all stitched with gold.
> On her gentle back she carried
> a little gerbil with a cold.
>
> Ah-choo!

Curricular Goals for "Golden Giraffe and Cinnamon Cat"

Following is a list of possible curricular goals to be accomplished with this poem. You need not spend a lesson on each goal. Devote your lessons to meeting those curricular goals that will best serve your particular class.

- introductory work
- focus on comprehension
- building confidence and community
- focus on developing an ear for rhyme
- focus on spelling patterns
- focus on sight words

Testing the Rules for c and g: A Lesson Using
"Golden Giraffe and Cinnamon Cat"

Primary Curricular Goals

- focus on spelling patterns: soft and hard *c*, soft and hard *g*

Previously Covered

- introductory work
- focus on comprehension
- building confidence and community
- focus on developing an ear for rhyme

Setup

- Before the lesson, create rule charts for *c* and *g* (see Figures 3–4 and 3–5). Post the charts so that children can see them as you read the poem.

- You may want to have previously identified and marked with color-coded transparent tape each instance of a word containing hard and soft *c* and *g* in the poem.

- Gather your students together on the rug or at your class meeting place so that they will all be able to see the words of the poem.

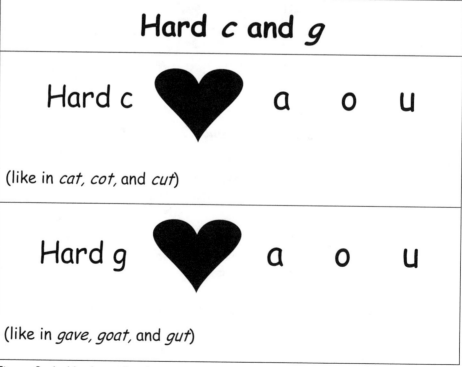

Figure 3–4 *Hard c and g chart*

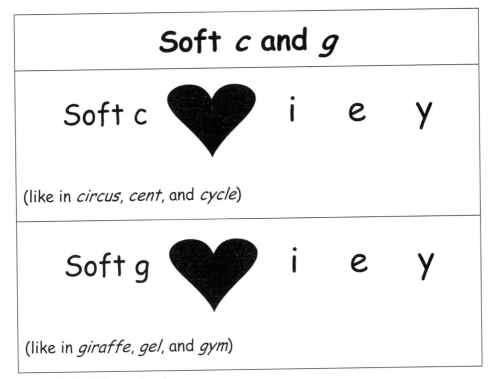

Soft *c* and *g*

Soft *c* ♥ *i* *e* *y*

(like in *circus*, *cent*, and *cycle*)

Soft *g* ♥ *i* *e* *y*

(like in *giraffe*, *gel*, and *gym*)

Figure 3–5 *Soft* c *and* g *chart*

Introduction

■ Tell your students that after you read the poem once through together, you'll be testing out the rules for hard and soft *c* and *g* words on the words you've identified in the poem. Show them the rule charts and explain that the charts may help them remember that most of the time, *c* and *g* make the hard sound when they are next to the vowels *a*, *o*, and *u*. Most of the time they make the soft sound when they are next to the vowels *e*, *i*, and *y*. Tell them that because you want to make sure the rules are correct, you want the students to help you test them out.

Interacting with the Text

■ Read the poem through with your class, asking the students to pay particular attention to the *c* and *g* words in the poem.
■ After you have read the poem through, model identifying a *c* or *g* word in the poem and then testing it against the rule.
■ Ask for student volunteers to identify a word and check it against the rules.
■ When you have finished testing all of the words, discuss with your students whether or not they think that the rules hold true.

Extending Your Class' Work with "Golden Giraffe and Cinnamon Cat"

■ Have students test out the rules in their independent reading. Invite them to keep a list on a sticky note as they read that they can report on later when the class comes back together. Have they found exceptions to the rule? Does every rule have an exception?

■ Have your students invent and envision their own circus. A cat on a bike with a carrot in his hat is not the most common of circus acts, nor is a giraffe in a gold gown bearing a sick gerbil! Can your students think of some other silly circus acts? You may have them write their own circus poems or stories to illustrate, or you may decide to do this collaboratively.

2

Homophones: *to, too, two*
Sight words: *also, and, are, but, by, for, go, good, is, isn't, it, it's, just, like, may, more, much, same, than, that, the, them, they, she, so, to, too, two, up, when, where, will, you, your, you've*

2
It's true
that to
and too
and two
are spoken just the same.

To tells where.
Too means also.
Two is more than one by one.

And when you talk
it's good to know
they sound alike.
But when you write
it isn't right
to mix them up.
Go slow.

To Mom,
I'd like two cookies
for myself
and two for teddy, too.

(Your mom will think
you've learned so much
she may give them to you.)
—*Amy Ludwig VanDerwater*

Curricular Goals for "2"

Following is a list of possible curricular goals to be accomplished with this poem. You need not spend a lesson on each goal. Devote your lessons to meeting those curricular goals that will best serve your particular class.

- introductory work
- focus on comprehension
- building confidence and community
- focus on homophones
- focus on sight words

Memorization and Recitation: A Lesson Using "2"

Primary Curricular Goals

- focus on comprehension
- building confidence and community
- focus on homophones: *to, too, two*

Previously Covered

- introductory work

Setup

- You want to have read this poem through many times already so your students know it well; some may already have memorized the poem.

- Gather your students together on the rug or at your class meeting place so that they will all be able to see the words of the poem.

- Have available a large piece of paper or a file folder or something you can use to cover the words of the poem as you practice memorizing it with your class.

Introduction

- Tell your students that because Amy's poem "2" is such a good teacher all on its own, it will be really helpful if they can memorize it and have it in their heads always, so that when they are writing they can use it to help them remember which word they need.

Interacting with the Text

- Ask your students to read the poem with you once through.
- Cover up the first stanza of the poem and ask them to say it by memory. You may need to give them the first couple of words to get started.
- After reciting the first stanza together, check it with the words.
- Cover up the second stanza and do the same thing; continue until you've practiced each stanza in isolation.

- Cover the entire poem and attempt to recite the whole thing with your class. This may take some prompting!
- You'll probably need to practice this over the course of a few days—it is a long poem.

From the Classroom: Incorporating Poetry Language into Your Shared Reading Discussions

While shared reading is often used for the purpose of reinforcing sight words and spelling patterns as well as practicing various reading skills rather than teaching about the craft of poetry, Elizabeth likes to incorporate poetry vocabulary and ideas into all of her shared reading lessons, particularly early on when children are discussing what they notice about the poem and what it means. Elizabeth's class of second graders is already in the habit of referring to stanzas of the poem and to noticing line breaks, repetition, rhyme, and comparison (simile or metaphor). While Elizabeth may not focus a lot of time during shared reading on exploring those concepts, she finds that knowing them helps her students become much more specific and informed when they are talking about the shared reading poems together. For example, when helping her students consider changes from stanza to stanza in one poem, it helps that her students have the word "stanza" as part of their common vocabulary. One student notices, "In the first stanza, it feels slow and sort of quiet because the lines are so short you have to read really slowly. The other stanzas have longer lines, like the person is thinking faster and faster about *to*, *too*, and *two*."

Extending Your Class' Work with "2"

- Ask your students to write several sentences that contain all three homophones. You may want to provide them with an example or two: "I want to go to the store and get two treats, too!" or "Two boys swam to the other side of the lake, and they swam back, too!"

A Tall Tale

Homophones: *be, bee; hair, hare; tail, tale*
Sight words: *a, and, as, at, be, beautiful, for, from, he, his, I'll, in, just, little, not, of, so, the, was*

A Tall Tale
Of the hair on his tail,
the hare was so proud.
"So sweet! So soft!
Like a little white cloud!"
He gazed at his tail
as he hopped along.
He admired his tail.
He sang a tail song:
"I'll sing you the tale
of a beautiful tail
as white and as clean
as a billowing sail."
As he hopped, he looked backwards—
so he didn't see
he was hopping directly
towards the hive of a bee.
The ending is sad for the hare—not the bee.
The bee shouted "Be careful!"
But it wasn't to be.
From ear-tip to tail-end
the hare was covered in honey,
and his cloudy white tail
just looked sticky and funny.

Curricular Goals for "A Tall Tale"

Following is a list of possible curricular goals to be accomplished with this poem. You need not spend a lesson on each goal. Devote your lessons to meeting those curricular goals that will best serve your particular class.

- introductory work
- focus on comprehension
- building confidence and community
- focus on developing an ear for rhyme
- focus on homophones
- focus on sight words

Homophone Guessing Game: A Lesson Using "A Tall Tale"

Primary Curricular Goals

- focus on homophones: *be, bee; hair, hare; tail, tale*

Previously Covered

- introductory work
- focus on comprehension
- building confidence and community
- developing an ear for rhyme

Setup

- Before the lesson, you'll want to have made a list of the homophones appearing in the poem with your class and either added on others yourself or extended the list with your class, depending on their facility with homophones.

- Type up a list of the homophones you've collected and make a copy for each student.

- Gather your students together on the rug or at your class meeting place so that they will all be able to see the words of the poem.

Introduction

- Tell your students that after you read the poem through together, paying particular attention to the homophones in it, you'll be looking over your class list of homophones, and then they'll be working in partnerships on a homophone guessing game.

Interacting with the Text

- Read the poem through with your class.

■ Read your class list of homophones or have a student volunteer read through it. As a review, ask students to define a few of the homophones before you send them off to work.

■ Tell your students that they will be working with their reading partners (or in other partnerships as you see fit) to play a homophone guessing game. They'll each get a copy of the homophone list, and they will take turns choosing a homophone and using it in a sentence. The other partner will then, using his copy of the list, if he likes, decide which of the homophones his partner has used in the sentence. Then the partners will switch roles.

■ Model this process for your students, using a student as your partner. For example, you might choose the word *hair* and say the sentence, "The girl braided her hair." Have your student partner guess which spelling—*hair* or *hare*—you have used.

■ Send your students off in pairs to play the game. Have them continue as long as seems reasonable for your class.

From the Classroom: Tips for Managing Partner Work

Managing small-group and partner work can be a challenge: What are they all really doing? Are they really playing the game? Are they really talking about their books? Partner work is such an important part of classroom work, both in terms of the practice it provides students with the content and with interacting with a peer—making decisions, negotiating conflicts, and so on—but children need to be much more aware of self-regulating because they are expected to work more independently. Sometimes a little extra structure and very explicit instructions can create a sturdy platform from which students can work on their own. Before sending her students off to play the homophone guessing game in partnerships, Helen sets them up clearly so that they know exactly what to do. She has found that with this particular class, it is really important to set them up and to support them along the way; otherwise, partners begin to lose focus quickly. As she calls each partnership off the rug to their work spots, she puts a red label dot on the hand of one of the partners. The children are familiar with this practice now, and they know that students with the dots on their hands will be coming up with the homophone sentences first. Helen has also asked the pairs not to start until every child is ready in her work seat, so that she can explain the next step. When everyone is sitting, she reminds the children with the dots what to do first and then has them begin. She has also told them that they may switch the dot to the other partner's hand when it is his turn. She checks in with the class after a few minutes by turning off the lights and quieting them and then asking them if everyone has had a chance to ask and to answer. When the game is finished, Helen will quiet the class again, and she will ask for a collector to pick up the dots before calling children back to their meeting spots.

■ Have each students choose a homophone pair and write her own tall tale featuring those words.

■ This poem is a good one for memorization and recitation because it tells a story and it is full of rhythm and rhyme.

■ Have your students act out the poem in pairs—they can even use the dialogue of the bee and the hare!

The Cake Isn't for Us

Contractions: *couldn't, didn't, don't, he'll, I'll, isn't, let's, she'll, she's, we'll, we've, won't, you'll*

Sight words: *and, even, ever, if, it, just, no, out, say, she, so, the, there, we, when, will, you*

> ### *The Cake Isn't for Us*
> Let's do and say we didn't.
> Well, we shouldn't.
> No, we couldn't!
> He'll try it. She'll try it.
> Won't you try it? Don't deny it!
> The cake she's baked
> looks so delicious
> sitting there alone.
> I'll try it if you'll try it.
> No one will ever know!
> We'll just even out the frosting
> when we've finished, nice and slow.
> Let's do, and say we didn't,
> if she asks.

Curricular Goals for "The Cake Isn't for Us"

Following is a list of possible curricular goals to be accomplished with this poem. You need not spend a lesson on each goal. Devote your lessons to meeting those curricular goals that will best serve your particular class.

- introductory work
- focus on comprehension
- building confidence and community
- focus on developing an ear for rhyme

- focus on contractions
- focus on sight words

Breaking Up Contractions: A Lesson Using "The Cake Isn't for Us"

Primary Curricular Goals:

- focus on contractions: *couldn't, didn't, don't, he'll, I'll, isn't, let's, she'll, she's, we'll, we've, won't, you'll*

Previously Covered

- introductory work
- focus on comprehension
- building confidence and community

Setup

- Gather your students together on the rug or at your class meeting place so that they will all be able to see the words of the poem.

- You may have spent time in a previous lesson having children notice and mark the contractions in the poem with colored transparent tape.

- Have a prepared blank chart or just leave space on your board so that children will be able to work on splitting contractions into the words they are made of. A blank chart might look like the one in Figure 3–6.

Contractions	
Contraction	Words

Figure 3–6 *Blank contractions chart*

Introduction

- Tell your students that after they read the poem together, paying particular attention to the contractions, you'll be examining together how the contractions are made and using the chart to help you.

Interacting with the Text

- Read the poem through once with your students.

- Choose a contraction from the poem to use as a model for your students. Write the contraction—say, *isn't*—in the top-left space. Ask your students to tell you what words the contraction is made up of and what letter(s) the apostrophe represents. Write *is not* in the top-right space.

- Ask individual students to choose a contraction from the poem and then come up to add the contraction to the chart. (See the sample partially completed chart in Figure 3–7.)

- Keep the finished chart visible in the room for students to use when they are reading and writing.

Contractions	
Contraction	Words
isn't	is not
let's	let us
he'll	he will

Figure 3–7 *Partially completed contractions chart*

Postcard from Someplace Lopsided

Compound words: *afternoon, anything, awestruck, beehives, buttercup, butterflies, downpour, heartbeat, ladybugs, lopsided, moonbeam, postcard, rosebud, seashores, sideways, somebody, someplace, something, starlight, sunflowers, sunrise, sweetheart, wheelbarrow, wishbone*

Sight words: *a, all, am, and, anything, be, but, could, do, from, full, have, here, I, I'd, in, is, it, just, love, my, of, on, see, so, somebody, something, the, this, to, you*

Postcard from Someplace Lopsided
Dear Sweetheart,

I have spent the afternoon
watching the sunrise.
All is sideways but full of butterflies.
Here, the ladybugs live in beehives
and the sunflowers bloom on seashores.
Oh, it is something!
Just this morning,
sipping my tea from a buttercup
and basking in a moonbeam,
I heard the heartbeat of a rosebud.
I'd do anything if you could be here
to see the wheelbarrows of wishbones
and the downpour of starlight.
Please visit soon.
I am awestruck but oh so lonely.

Love,
Somebody Blue

—Nicole Callihan

Curricular Goals for "Postcard from Someplace Lopsided"

Following is a list of possible curricular goals to be accomplished with this poem. You need not spend a lesson on each goal. Devote your lessons to meeting those curricular goals that will best serve your particular class.

- introductory work
- focus on comprehension
- building confidence and community
- focus on developing an ear for rhyme
- focus on compound words
- focus on sight words

Compound Word Cards: A Lesson Using "Postcard from Someplace Lopsided"

Primary Curricular Goals

- focus on compound words

Previously Covered

- introductory work
- focus on comprehension
- building confidence and community

Setup

- Before the lesson, prepare a cardstock card for each child. If you cut an 8½-by-11-inch piece of cardstock in half vertically, you can make two cards. Fold each side in toward the center so that you have two equally sized "doors" that open up.

- Also prepare a completed sample card to show your students.

- You will want to have read the poem through together several times already, and you may want to have had your students identify the compound words in the poem as well, either with transparent colored tape or by writing up a list.

- Gather your students together on the rug or at your class meeting place so that they will all be able to see the words of the poem.

Introduction

- Tell your students that after you read the poem through together, you'll be doing a project using compound words. Remind them that a compound word is when two words are put together to make a brand-new word, like *baseball* and *watermelon*. Tell them that they'll be using the cards you've prepared to pay attention to how compound words are made.

Interacting with the Text

■ After reading the text through together, review the compound words in the poem. You could have students identify compound words they see in the poem and also have them identify which two words are put together to make each compound word.

■ Show your students the cards you've prepared, and explain that each child will be choosing a compound word (either one from Nicole's poem or one that the child thinks of on his own) to write on the doors of the card. Explain that they will write one part of the compound word on one door and the other part on the other door. For example, if a student chose the word *watermelon*, *water* would be written on the left door and *melon* would be written on the right, so that the two matched up when the doors were closed. Explain that when the doors are opened up, the students will draw a picture that represents the compound word in the space inside. It is helpful to have a finished sample to show students at this point as well. See Figures 3–8 and 3–9.

Figure 3–8

Figure 3–9

■ Have your students decide on the compound words they are going to use before sending them to their work seats to get started.

■ Students will be excited to share their words with each other. You may even want to hang these all up in your room or on a bulletin board.

From the Classroom: Tips for Inclusion—the Child Who Can't Stop Talking When Called On

Fiona is an enthusiastic and engaged second grader who always has something to add to class discussions. She is particularly informed about the world and loves to share her insights with the class; she recently explained how snow is made, for example. She also loves to tell the class about her experiences with her family outside of school. When called on, Fiona often has a very hard time ending her thought and moving on. One thought leads to another thought, which leads into a story, and soon Fiona is off to the races! She seems almost impelled to finish these stories, and it is hard for her teacher, Bonnie, to get her to stop. Simply asking her to stop so that someone else can speak doesn't work—Fiona will just keep talking over her teacher. Using a stern voice hasn't helped either—Fiona seems to know that she should stop but can't quite get herself to do it. For example, early on in a conversation with the class about the compound words in Nicole's poem, when Bonnie called on Fiona to notice a compound word in the poem, Fiona said, "*Wheelbarrow* is a compound word, and my grandpa has one in the shed, and when I went to visit him he let me ride in it, and we went out to the garden and we were taking away the old plants, and . . ." She continued for a few sentences even when Bonnie reminded her firmly to just answer the question.

Bonnie has been thinking about how to help Fiona with this. She doesn't like the feeling of raising her voice as Fiona speaks, and she sees that it is not helping at all. She decides to try something different: instead of waiting to correct Fiona until she is already in the full swing of her answer, Bonnie decides to preview what is expected with her before Fiona starts to answer a question. This way, Fiona starts talking with a clearer plan for herself. Later in the discussion about Nicole's poem, Bonnie calls on Fiona again.

"Fiona, before you answer the question, I want to remind you about something: we are *only* noticing compound words right now, and then saying what two words they are made of. So think for a second before you answer; you are going to only say a compound word and the two words it's made of, and then it will be someone else's turn. OK?"

"OK," Fiona says. "*Butterfly* is one. It's *butter* and *fly* together." The girl pauses for a moment and then starts to continue. "And . . ."

"Oops!" interrupts Bonnie with a smile. "Remember, just the word. You did it! Now it's someone else's turn. Hank?"

Bonnie gives Fiona a thumbs-up and a grin as the conversation continues.

■ Have your students write their own postcards from someplace lopsided. You may want to brainstorm a list of compound words they can use in their poems before you send them off.

■ Write each of the compound words in Nicole's poem on an index card. Have children cut the cards in half in between each of the two words that make up the compound word. You may also have them reassemble compound words using the cut-apart cards.

Writing and Collecting Poems for Your Class

■ Writing Poems for Shared Reading

The idea for this book took shape in my mind because I wanted poems that fit my own students' specific needs. There are countless wonderful poems written for children out there in the world, as well as several anthologies of poems to be used for the purposes of shared reading. But I was having trouble finding exactly what I needed, so I started to write my own. The poems in this book are designed with many children's needs in mind, not just my own students', and they're based on a generally agreed-upon sequence of instruction, but only you know exactly what your class is ready for and exactly when.

I encourage you to try writing your own poems for use with your class. Children love being the subject of poems, and they love to know that you have made something just for them. Writing shared reading poems for your class is not as daunting as it may initially seem. I started making mine up on my walk to school in the mornings. For example, I knew I'd be teaching the *ank, ink, onk,* and *unk* patterns in word study the following week, so I'd walk down Seventh Avenue in Brooklyn past the early-morning dog walkers, little piles of dry ice steaming amid an ice-cream delivery, pigeons swooping and banking around rooftops, and I'd think, *ink. Pink, think, blink, wink, sink. Link. Rink. Stink. Slink.* A little rhyming litany as I walked. When I'm writing a poem to promote a particular spelling pattern, I go through this process almost every time—though not always as I walk down Seventh Avenue!

Let me take you through the process from start to finish, using the poem "Sam's Map," which was designed to feature the short *a* spelling patterns *am, ap,* and *at.* Here's the poem as it appears in the book, near the end of Chapter 1.

> **Sam's Map**
> My friend Sam
> loves his subway map.
> He's happy that he has one.
> He looks at his map

before his nap.
He looks at his map
with his family.
He rests his map upon his lap
and imagines the trains underground:
zooming around with a wham and a slam
past rats and bats
and little lost cats.
Sam loves his subway map!

I had no idea what the poem would be about before I started working on it. I wrote the three spelling patterns I had in mind, *am*, *ap*, and *at*, at the top of my journal page and then wrote quick lists of words that contained each pattern. The lists looked like this:

am	*ap*	*at*
bam	cap	bat
dam	gap	cat
family	happy	fat
ham	lap	hat
jam	map	mat
lamb	nap	pat
ram	rap	rat
Sam	sap	sat
wham	tap	
yam	wrap	
slam	trap	
	slap	
	chap	

I could have kept going, and I am sure you are thinking of many more words that fit those patterns as you read. When I feel I've got enough words to go on, I stop and start looking at the lists. I look for words that are simple and appealing to kids. I look for words that might allow for a silly or engaging situation to come to life in a poem. As I was reading these lists, I remembered a little boy in my class years ago who was absolutely enamored of the subway and subway maps. His name was not in fact Sam, but that didn't matter, for the purposes of the poem. With *Sam* and *map*, I already had two examples of short *a*.

When I've got a concept in mind, as I did with "Sam's Map" at this point, I dive in, reassuring myself that I can always stop and try something completely different if it doesn't work. I wrote:

> My friend Sam
> loves the subway map.
> He keeps it . . .

And then I stopped. I wondered if there might be a way to get in another short *a* word. I crossed off the bottom line and added:

> He's happy
> that he has one.

Happy and *that*—two more! I kept going, referring back to my lists.

> My friend Sam
> loves the subway map.
> He's happy
> that he has one.
> He looks at his map
> before his nap.
> He looks at his map
> with his family.

Sounded OK so far. I'd gotten in *nap, family,* and a couple more instances of *map*; it is helpful to repeat the same word a few times, too—when you have children hunt in the poem for that word, they have opportunities to track the print and find it in several places.

So now I've got Sam showing his map to everyone, looking at it before his nap . . . let's have him wake up, I thought. I added:

> When he wakes up
> he pretends he takes the Q.

I thought about that for a moment—people outside of New York City wouldn't get the reference to a particular train, so that might not be the most universally useful line. Also, there were no short *a* words to be seen. Back to the list—how about *lap?* I wrote:

> He rests his map upon his lap
> when he's at the dinner table.
> He imagines the trains
> staying dry in the rain
> zooming below with a wham and a slam
> past rats and bats and folks in hats,
> Sam loves his subway map.

It seemed to be getting there, but more revision was in order. Much as I enjoyed the idea of trains being dry as it rained outside, that part didn't add any short *a* words to the mix, and I didn't want the poem to become too long and wordy—why not cut to the chase? I also decided that people in hats are not often hanging out deep in the subway tunnels with the bats and the rats—and if they were, I need not mention it in a poem for little kids! I made two changes, and the last section became:

> He rests his map upon his lap
> And imagines the trains underground:
> zooming around with a wham and a slam
> past rats and bats
> and little lost cats.
> Sam loves his subway map.

Finally, I read the completed poem through a few times to myself to make sure it had an engaging rhythm and that children would be able to catch on quickly to both the concept and the words.

You can do this, too! Your children will *love* to know that you've written a poem for them. They'll be delighted if you work their names into the poem as well or refer to experiences the class has had together. Nothing engages children more in a poem than feeling connected to it, and they can't help but be connected to poems that are all about them. I haven't included poems of this nature in this book because they are tailored to specific classes, but here's an example from several years ago. My class of kindergartners went on an ill-fated trip to the Brooklyn Bridge—about halfway across the bridge, the skies suddenly and dramatically opened up on us. Everyone's umbrella turned inside out, and we rushed through the squall back to our waiting bus. Once back at school, all of the kids changed into whatever extra clothes we had, a parent chaperone rushed home to bring back more, and we cozied up and ate snacks and read stories on the rug for the rest of the afternoon. Later on, I wrote this poem for them:

Bridge Adventure

It was sunny when we started.
The skies were very bright.
The towers of the Brooklyn Bridge
Stood tall and straight with all their might!

We saw the anchorage,
we saw the cables.
We saw the towers—
but then the weather turned the tables!

The winds rushed in.
The sky turned black.

With our inside-out umbrellas,
K-118 went rushing back!

Some of us were scared,
and some of us were worried.
Towards our waiting yellow bus
K-118 hurried!

All except for Ivan,
who would much rather stay.
In his bright red slicker,
he was dancing in the rain!

While this poem is longer than a poem I might typically use early on in shared reading, the children were absolutely engaged by it. We all laughed together about how Ivan was the last one off the bridge and how he smiled and danced all the way to the bus. The poem was a bit too sophisticated for the word work we were doing at that point in kindergarten, but it was useful in terms of simply reading together and practicing fluency and expression. There several familiar word wall words in the poem as well—*and, the, was,* and *he,* to name a few.

Give it a try: when you are planning your word work, see if you might make up a little poem that features the words or patterns you plan to study. Your students will love it, and your poem will support them as they learn something new!

■ Collecting Poems for Shared Reading

In addition to writing your own poems for your class, keep your ears open and your eyes peeled for appropriate poems you might come across throughout your days. PS 321 assistant principal Beth Handman offered a wonderful little poem using the homophones *there, they're,* and *their:*

There goes the rain
What is in those drops?
They're perfect tears, in perfect patterns,
with their perfect rhythms.

In addition to the countless wonderful children's poems out there, often poems written by older children in your school can be really useful for teaching sight words in particular. The older kids are usually delighted to share their poems, and younger children will love studying poems that were written by children just a few years older than themselves. If your school has a reading buddy program that matches lower-grade classes with upper-grade classes, you may even invite the older kids to write some poems specifically for your students. If this doesn't seem like a workable plan for the whole class, you might commission a poem or two from interested older students.

■ Using Your Students' Poems

As I worked on this project and tried out poems in my own classroom, initially I didn't tell the children that many of the poems we studied were poems that I'd made up myself. Because these poems were designed to apply to *many* classrooms, not just my own, I didn't want their responses to be influenced by knowing I'd written them. At one point, however, as my class was discussing the poem "Backyard Digging," Will raised his hand to ask what the kid in the poem *actually found* in the dirt in the backyard. He said, "The author only says what the kid is imagining; he doesn't say what's actually in there." I asked Will to tell us what *he* thought might be in the dirt. Will replied, "I don't know!" as though I'd asked a completely ridiculous question. He then added, "The author should tell us. The author should write another poem!"

This provided a great opportunity for me to let the kids in on my secret. "Well," I said, "you have asked the right person those questions, Will. Guess who wrote this poem? I did!" The kids looked astounded. Some of them giggled. I explained that I'd been working on a poem project and that I was trying to write poems that helped kindergartners and other kids practice learning words. Elena asked if that's why the poems had so many word wall words in them, and I told her she'd hit the nail on the head. She immediately made a plan to write some poems of her own for the class to use during shared reading as well! Before we moved on, I asked Will if he'd like me to write another poem that would answer his question, and he (and the rest of the class) enthusiastically agreed. Here it is—an answer to Will's question:

> I dug, I dug, I dug.
> I found so many bugs!
> I found an old boot
> and a ring
> and a root.
> But the very best thing
> was the pirate loot
> I found when I dug
> and I dug.

The very next day, Elena made good on her promise. She had indeed caught the spirit and gone home to write, with her mommy, a poem containing several of our class' sight words. (See Figure 4–1.) We studied Elena's poem that day during shared reading time, and it was wonderful to watch her beam with pride as the kids read her work together. If kids in your class catch the spirit as Elena did, support them! I always aspire to help build a classroom environment in which children have ownership of and are full participants in their own learning. After we studied Elena's poem, several other students said that they planned to make their own poems as well.

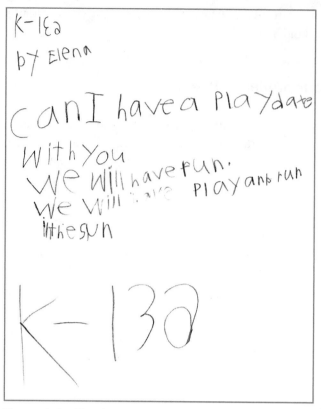

Figure 4–1 *Elena's poem*

While I hope the poems appearing in this book provide a sequence and frame-work to use for shared reading work, I also hope that you and your students will find ways to play with poems together in ways that are specific to your own class-rooms. Write poems for your students! Read poems by your students! Invite in guest poets! Play!